MONEY
MYTHS AND REALITIES

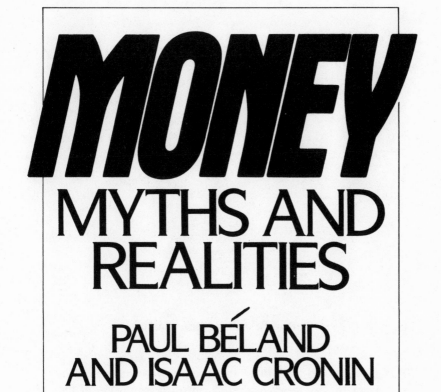

MONEY
MYTHS AND REALITIES

PAUL BÉLAND
AND ISAAC CRONIN

Carroll & Graf Publishers, Inc.
New York

First Carroll & Graf edition 1986

Carroll & Graf Publishers, Inc.
260 Fifth Avenue
New York, NY 10001

Library of Congress Cataloging-in-Publication Data

Béland, Paul.
  Money myths and realities.

  1. Money.   I. Cronin, Isaac, 1948–
II. Title.
HG221.B425   1986   332.4   86-12886
ISBN: 0-88184-265-6

Manufactured in the United States of America

ACKNOWLEDGEMENTS

We would like to thank the following people for their help and support: Richard Sasnow for putting us up; Richard Chambers for his useful suggestions; Terrel Seltzer and Clair Thiebaud for their unfailing senses of humor; Herman Graf for leading us to Sammy's Rumanian Steak House; and Kent Carroll for sending us our checks on time; and Michel Delisle for telling us we were on the right track.

CONTENTS _____

Introduction

THERE IS NO way to ignore money, no way to live without it. Money, like sex, is a subject around which a void never exists, which generates excitement, passion, and heated debate. Just as sexual desire asserts itself whether or not people are ready to accept it, money is a powerful and irrepressible social force with which everyone must come to terms whether they want to or not. Since this is the case, since we all live in a world where money is clearly the single most powerful factor affecting individual as well as collective actions, we have assumed that an intelligent and comfortable relationship with money based on an understanding of what it is and what it does is a worthwhile goal.

The major obstacle to full and profitable participation in modern life is not the lack of formal education, of proper family background, or of political acumen, but the lack of money literacy. Money illiteracy, an inadequate understanding of money fundamentals, of what money is and what it does, is far more widespread than functional illiteracy and cuts across all social and economic categories. We intend to show that some deeply ingrained and commonly held misconceptions about money, which we have dubbed *the money myths*, are the bedrock of this illiteracy, which leads people to take up attitudes detrimental to money and to use it in ways which are often damaging both for themselves and for society.

The Money Myths

The money myths are as ubiquitous as money itself, and are part and parcel of what is erroneously considered common sense, at least in North America. These myths are the stuff of corporate boardroom presentations, street corner and dining room conversations, newspaper and magazine headlines, politicians' speeches and economists' lectures everywhere. Among other things, the money mythology holds as self-evident truths that money causes wars, that it is vulgar, that it is best understood by experts, that it fosters inequalities and resists social change.

This leads us to the heart of the book. Each chapter begins with the presentation of a myth ("The Myth") and the examination of some of the most blatantly unfortunate attitudes and events caused by belief in that myth ("The Myth in Action"). We then proceed to refute the myth both by taking a close look at the historical development of money and by reexamining current events from the perspective of money ("The Myth Unraveled"). Finally, we point out some trends and effects of the new money awareness, the concrete ways in which people are changing their relationship to money as money itself changes, and, where appropriate, we draw conclusions about the foreseeable impact of the spreading of these attitudes ("Toward Money Literacy").

Caveat Reader

There may be dozens of false ideas about money, but there is no simple definition of money, no single sentence or paragraph, no magic formula which sums up what money is. The definition of money which emerges from our research is multifaceted and complex. At the beginning of his classic book *Money: Whence It Came, Where It Went*, John Kenneth Galbraith tried to reassure his readers that "money is nothing more or less than what he or she always thought it was—what is commonly offered or received for the purchase or sale of goods, services or other things."[1] In our opinion this outlook is both limited and limiting. Our feeling is that money is everything you always thought it was and then some; Money is at once the stuff that dreams are made on *and* the essential ingredient for turning dreams into reality. Of course money is, as all the experts have said, the prime means of exchange. Indeed, for most people the most immediate image which the term *money* conjures up is that of currency, money you can actually touch; but if currency is money, money is not only, or mainly, currency. Currency fascinates and exerts a powerful attraction because, being money, it shares some of the power of money, the prime mover of social events worldwide. While the technicalities of money as a means of exchange have been discussed in considerable detail by many authors, the role of money as a determinant force in shaping our lives has been almost completely ignored. This is the gap in our understanding of money which we hope to help fill.

Confronting Money Illiteracy and Money Guilt

Coming to terms with money illiteracy, confronting one's endorsement of the money myths and of the attitudes based on them, is no easy task. Misconceptions which are fundamental and deeply rooted have a large emotional legacy attached to them, and the subject of money is probably the most emotionally charged of all. (For example, it is commonly acknowledged that most marital disputes revolve around two topics: sex and money, with money currently getting top billing.) Therefore, one must approach the subject most carefully. Borrowing from the method and language of psychoanalysis, we found that just as misunderstandings about sex, repressed sexual desires, hesitant sexual practices, and shame provoked guilt in vast numbers of reasonably normal people at the turn of the century, inadequate knowledge about money and the resulting ambivalent and self-limiting money practices have caused most people to feel apprehensive and guilty toward money. Nowhere is the uneasiness about money more clearly expressed than in this widespread phenomenon of money guilt. Guilt is one of the best adaptive mechanisms around; it allows the expression and even the embellishment of a problem without altering the circumstances which produce it. Once people become accustomed to feeling money guilt, they include it in the price they have to pay for getting things done. They take it for granted that they will feel somewhat uneasy when they make money, and they expect those whom they deal with will feel uncomfortable, too.

One clear measure of money guilt is how much time we all spend making excuses for the money we have and what we do with it: it doesn't do to be only in it for the money and to say so. One does not just make money; one is saving for this or that noble cause, such as a child's education or enriching the community with a much needed service. Getting a windfall is somehow seen as a deserved reward, as simply being paid a proper wage for all those years of being underpaid. A European vacation is not simply a wonderful thing to do, but necessary for our business education or the kid's cultural upbringing. No matter what the situation, one always hears about the inconveniences and traumas first, the fun later, if ever. The same goes for the *au pair*. Few would dare say, "We don't have to do housework because we make enough money to pay someone else to do it and ain't it grand," without launching an avalanche of ugly stares and malicious gossip. Instead, we hear the cliché, "It's so hard [i.e., such hard work] to get good help." Another sign of money guilt is that people insist on the sacrifices they had to make to get their money in the first place. We constantly hear of: endless hours, long and exhausting trips away from home, mean office politics, even the pain of those embarrassing meetings to request salary increases.

Money guilt is not restricted to the affluent: it affects

men and women of all income levels. Many people without money simply opt out of the pursuit of it because they feel guilty about even dreaming of money, of wanting it. These people are prime targets for the money-hate propaganda disseminated by the money moralists: the political and religious movements ranging from Marxists to Christian fundamentalists to Moslems.

Money Guilt on Wall Street

Money guilt has undoubtedly been around for a long time, but until recently its presence was covered up by another, more pressing problem: namely, that thirty years ago, just getting enough money to get by was the overriding, pressing concern of the overwhelming majority of people. Today, feeling uncomfortable with money is as big a problem for some people as simply obtaining enough money to get by has traditionally been for others. Self-sabotage, a peculiar form of money guilt, is now recognized as a major element in many career failures.

A great many people, to judge from their behavior, really don't want to succeed. Executives and supervisors—subconsciously to be sure—often seem to choose the one road on which the signposts seem to point to defeat. Sooner or later they turn their triumphs into disasters. When things go well they consider themselves unworthy of their good fortune and therefore strive to undo it.[2]

Pop psychologists, when they explain self-sabotage, usually attribute it to personal weakness. For various reasons, ranging from the faulted upbringing of women to the male repressed fear of usurping the father, it is always the individual's inability to accept success which is at fault. As anyone can tell, success, first and foremost, consists of money and of the ability to come to grips with it. But a discussion of why people would reject money has so far not been deemed appropriate. The only approach to the problems of self-sabotage has been one of hastily designed coping strategies such as the "learning to take yourself seriously because you are a worthwhile person at heart" school of personal boosterism.

Collective Money Guilt Rituals

Society is full of collective expressions of money guilt as well. Probably the best known of these rituals is Hollywood's Academy Awards ceremonies where thousands of millionaires each year vote to bestow a number of Oscars on the film which most vividly portrays the life of the poor and even points an accusing finger at the rich. In the same vein, televised appeals for the needy abound, including the current campaigns for the hungry of Africa and the bankrupt farmers of America. The plight of these people is nearly always presented as some kind of accident of nature (the Africans would be fine except for the drought, the high grain prices, and the whims of their authoritarian governments, while the farmers would be doing okay except for uncontrollable government policies and the unfortunate good weather which makes for record crops and falling grain prices), not as the eminently avoidable result of unintelligent money practices which severely deprive some people of access to money. The main function of these events—as can be measured most concretely by the amount of money raised, which is nearly always pitiful compared with the amount required to solve the particular problem—is to give everyone involved a sense that something is being done while assuaging the money guilt of the organizers and contributors.

The Rewards of Money Literacy

Tackling money illiteracy is the key step in dispelling money guilt. Once the money mythology is unraveled, it is no longer necessary to feel bad about making money or about enjoying it. Although the lack of money may still be a problem for the money literate, just as the lack of sexual partners sometimes troubles the sexually well adjusted, money itself no longer constitutes a major source of guilt or discomfort. Money literacy can also be a tool for success in the following sense: unlike the "self-sabotager," who doesn't think he is worthy of success and who undercuts his own performance, the money-literate individual has eliminated a major source of self-doubt and can thus pursue his projects without fear that he is taking advantage of others or kidding himself about what his motives for making money are. And, finally, an understanding of money, the fundamental force in modern society, can only improve one's grasp on social reality as a whole.

Money Literacy and the Baby Boom Generation

Today, the closest thing we have to money literacy is the open-minded approach to money practiced by our generation, the baby boomers. We have evolved these new attitudes, not because of some special talent, but largely because we have grown up in a world in which money is ever present, and we have had no choice but to make our peace with money. For the baby boom generation money is not an adjunct, an incidental reward for a job well done, or a fascinating hobby; it is a central reference point for all of our public activity and private dreams. This emphasis on money is not the result of some kind of obsession or of tunnel vision, but is a reflection of healthy and straightforward approach to life.

The instant success and the nastiness of the yuppie caricature give an indication of how different from past attitudes this new openness to money is. Though the yuppie is attacked from all directions for being a self-centered, pretentious conformist, these barbs are just sociological and economic rationalizations for what is essentially moral outrage at this generation's new candid stance toward money. This self-righteous uproar, like the puritanical reaction to the changes in sexual behavior which began in the 1920s, is an attempt to discount momentous changes in collective attitudes. The older generation assumes that open money attitudes can only be inspired by the greed and pettiness which characterized many of those who sought affluence thirty, forty, and fifty years ago. Yuppies are not simply singled out because of their white-collar jobs or their consumption habits. Their most distinctive trait and the one their critics find most upsetting is their attitude toward money. The yuppies are those members of the baby boom generation who are not necessarily the most successful with money, but who are the most comfortable with money and who acknowledge its central role in their lives. We hope the yuppie label will fade away, not because people will get bored making fun of yuppies, but because this group's more healthy relation to money will become so commonplace as to be no longer newsworthy.

The Authors

Our generation has grown up in a complex and sophisticated world where rapid and visible changes were always the order of the day. Many of our own earliest childhood memories are of technological achievement— the pain from a shot of Salk vaccine, being called out to the yard at dusk to watch the early satellites pass overhead. Like many of our generation, we took scientific progress for granted. For us there were no such things as unconquerable diseases or inaccessible worlds. To this day the one thing that has constantly fascinated us is what holds together the social fabric of our down-to-earth world; what causes people to interact the way they do. Money is obviously the common denominator of all relationships, exchanges, and encounters in modern society, hence our curiosity about the subject.

Our approach to money differs dramatically from that of the money experts. Contemporary money literature, like current social science literature in general, is the work of credentialed specialists, experts who have earned their privileged positions by studying and mastering a particular theory or achieving success in a particular branch of expertise. This makes it easy to forget that the specialists' monopoly on social commentary is a recent development. Until World War II, the pronouncements of specialists about the evolution of society were usually regarded with skepticism, and the views of ordinary, well-informed people were taken seriously. The rising power of the scientific/technical community and the increasing centralization of the publishing industry, which brought editorial decision-making into fewer and less adventurous hands, greatly reduced the number of social commentaries written from a nonspecialist point of view. This is especially true where the treatment of money is concerned.

The shortcomings of the money literature are largely attributable to the field being dominated by specialists who, as we will soon discover, share an inherently limited point of view. Money is general, ubiquitous, and all-encompassing. But in the literature it is usually narrowly defined by economists who have theories to justify, by money managers, consultants, or figures from the corporate world who have their own investment or management strategies to defend, or by retired or aspiring politicians and civil servants with various axes to grind.

We are anything but money specialists; we are not even professional money commentators. Compared with the money specialists, we have no vested interest in tolerating money illiteracy. Like many members of the baby boom generation, we have gone from being full-time social gadflies in the sixties to full-time money earners (one a sound engineer, the other a nonfiction writer) in the seventies. In the process we jettisoned a passionate dislike for money in favor of a cautious respect for its power. We noticed our friends and associates, like ourselves, becoming more and more interested in money, not just in getting it but also in understanding it. But despite this massive pro-money movement which would provide an audience for an in-depth look at the subject, to say nothing of its broad appeal for other generations, we could find little progress in the study of money and its effects since the efforts of the classic economists of the eighteenth and nineteenth centuries. Rather than ask why, we decided why not, and plunged into the research ourselves. Our own money literacy has benefited greatly from this work; we hope our book has the same consequences for the reader.

—Money Myth 1:—

Money Is Best Understood by Experts

THE MYTH: In recent years the world of money has become far too complex to be fully understood by the average person. Deciphering the inner workings of money is best delegated to experts ranging from economists to money managers who, through systematic study, have managed to acquire an insider's view of *how money really works*, while the practical management of society is most competently carried out by politicians acting under the guidance of money experts.

The Myth in Action

The general public feel that there is a "world of money" beyond the realm of their common, everyday encounters with money; ordinary people feel uneasy about money because they lack the privileged insight into the world of money that successful business people, economists, financial experts, and professional money commentators have acquired through years of study and experience. Therefore, there is a tendency to defer to the experts' opinions and advice about money matters; and where public policy is concerned, power over matters of spending, taxation, and monetary policy are usually delegated outright.

If nothing else, the experts command respect; they are presumed to have a better perspective on money matters, and therefore on just about everything, because they are in a position to cultivate a multitude of personal contacts which give them access to "the inside dope."

There is such a strong notion that "the world of money" is more complicated than everyday life that people heed the experts' advice even when the most elementary common sense dictates otherwise. Most people feel utterly helpless when the time comes to invest or manage whatever money they have been smart enough to make. When they lose money because of financial decisions taken without expert advice, they feel guilty and they imagine it would have been otherwise had they been prudent enough to seek professional guidance. The same kind of syndrome affects the collectivity: seeking the money experts' opinions and second guesses on governments' budgets and policies is the national pastime of every Western country.

Even when it crosses the public mind that it is precisely the experts' advice which has brought about ruinous government deficits and has led oil producers, farmers, third-world countries and their bankers perilously close to an unprecedented precipice of defaults and bankruptcies, such a realization does not lead to a reconsideration of the state of money expertise. Rather than questioning the experts' assumptions, most members of the public simply conclude that, since the specialists themselves cannot fully understand and forecast money phenomena, a thorough understanding of money is probably an impossible dream, a hopeless quest. The dreadful consequence of such reasoning is that money, the most common, most central element of life, is further mystified and ultimately considered as absolutely imponderable.

The Myth Unraveled: Money, the Central Element of Everyday Life, Is the Most Natural Thing in the World

Money is so central to modern society that life without it is quite unthinkable. Money is at least as "natural" and almost as vital for people as the air they breathe or the food they eat. The nature and quality of the available air and food define, to a large extent, the quality of the physical environment in which different people live, but the quality of the human environment is determined by the relative presence or absence of money in a given society or in various sectors of a given society. The degree of freedom in a given country can generally be evaluated by looking at how freely money circulates in that country. Primitive or totalitarian countries have either little or no money, or severely restrict who can have access to money and under what circumstances. A foreign correspondent recently summed up the sad situation in the poverty-stricken, authoritarian-ruled African country of Mozambique: when he offered some "helping hand" a one-dollar tip, the potential recipient sadly refused and opted for two cigarettes instead, because there just was not enough money in the country for the reporter's dollar to mean anything. Immigration statistics seem to confirm this link between money and the quality of life: when given a choice, people will move to places where there is more money and more free circulation of money.

From the individual's point of view (the most "micro" of all the situations usually examined by "microeconomics," the study of the economy of small units), to live is to engage in monetary, or money-mediated, transactions. "Every step you take, every move you make" involves money, as a quick look at a typical morning routine reveals: You wake up (having a bed to sleep in or a place to stay involves some reference to money), you eat some food (which has to be paid for somehow), you step outside (provided there is no warrant out for your arrest for unpaid taxes or parking tickets), you buy a newspaper, and so on. The day has barely started and it has already been punctuated by a half-dozen or so money transactions or references to money.

In the real world the individual literally swims in a sea of money. People earn, spend, borrow, print, lend, steal, lose, and burn money; they worry about it, dream about it, think about it; they love it, need it, hate it, crave it; they kill for it, they die for it, they beg for it, they betray their country for it. Money is the omnipresent, constant, and overriding concern of every man and woman.

Money is the modern handshake. The contemporary greeting is, "Hi, I'm so-and-so and I make so much money." One doesn't ask, "How do you do?" It is much more to the point to ask your acquaintances how much money they are making: the answer to this question gives you a very good idea of just how well they are doing. Money is the modern rite of passage; money maturity is the hallmark of adulthood. In modern societies, to be an adult is to earn one's own money and to be able to make one's own decisions about one's own money.

There are, of course, some who quibble with money and who, out of despair or for ethical or ideological considerations, make every effort to live without money. But, try as they may, they invariably find out that they cannot live without reference to money; at most they can manage to survive without *legitimate* money. In fact, money remains the focal point of the money renegade's life, whether he or she lives on a would-be cashless agricultural commune or ekes out a living in some branch of the so-called underground economy. Circumventing money is a full-time job, and attempting to deny the power of money is in itself an attitude fully centered on money, if only negatively; saying no to something is to acknowledge its importance.

Money is people's overriding everyday concern, and justifiably so: when people talk and think about money, what they are considering is their entire life, their future, and the state and future of the world around them. This is just as true of societies as it is of individuals. In countries or sectors of society where there is little or no money, money is the *only* preoccupation, a true obsession, as witnessed by the proliferation of schemes to gain access to money, especially foreign hard currencies, through a multitude of black-market ploys, behind the Iron Curtain, in developing countries, or in any place where money is either scarce or severely regulated.

In the "big picture" of world trade and world affairs (known in learned circles as the domain of "macroeconomics"), the towering presence of money translates into striking statistics which only confirm the individual's perception of the importance of money. Money is so vital to the modern world that it is the most briskly traded item in the world. Consider for instance the trade in the most basic form of money, currency. The hottest trade item in the world is not gold, silver, plutonium, or any high-technology product; it is money. The volume of trade on the world's currency markets makes the total world trade figures seem puny: according to the *New York Times*, the world's foreign-exchange trading amounted to $35 trillion in 1984, while total world exports amounted to "only" $1.8 trillion. More significant, foreign-exchange trading has doubled in five years (from $17.5 trillion in 1979), while exports have grown by a mere 20 percent (from $1.5 trillion) during the same period. A current estimate is that the foreign-exchange markets handle some $150 billion a day, an amount roughly equivalent to 40 times the dollar value of the turnover of the New York Stock Exchange.[1] In other words, if the sums traded on the currency markets were used toward reducing the United States budget deficit, the current $200-billion deficit would be wiped out in less than two trading days. In this context, to say that money is an essential, everyday element of modern life is not an exaggeration; it almost sounds like an understatement.

The very magnitude of the sums involved at the macroeconomic level is sufficient to baffle most mortals. The man in the street deals with money and worries about it for most of his waking hours, and he probably dreams about it when he goes to bed. He is comfortable, even happy, when he has money and invariably miserable when deprived of it. Most of us take our own immediate relationship to money, however troubled it may be, pretty much for granted and we usually manage at least to "cope with it," if only one day at a time. But when confronted with large-scale money phenomena, the same individuals who are perfectly at ease with money in everyday situations often feel quite disoriented. One cannot help being overcome by a feeling of utter helplessness when trying to understand such large-scale money phenomena as the roller-coaster ride of interest rates or of commodity prices, the volatility of foreign-exchange rates or the periodic multiplication of bank failures. Governmental budget deficits, for instance, are so large that the numbers which describe them have come to mean almost nothing in absolute terms: public opinion perceives little difference between $400 billion and $600 billion, or between appropriations of $1.6 billion and $16 billion. Such figures only become understandable when they are explained in terms of the per capita national debt as it relates to the private citizen's own private money situation (as in, "Your share of the national debt is . . ." or "Every child born in this country already owes so-and-so much . . .").

However familiar it may be on a day-to-day basis and in "normal sums," say up to a few million dollars, money in the aggregate is still widely perceived as complex, unpredictable, and generally beyond the understanding of ordinary people. Individuals feel quite secure bathing in the sea of everyday money; but at the same time they feel like a cork tossed around on the troubled waters of the worldwide money turbulence. This dichotomy has given rise to one of the strangest situations of our time: for all practical purposes, people are more knowledgeable about atomic theory or the theory of universal gravitation than about the nature of money. Anyone can easily confirm this simply by asking any innocent bystander how money works, how it functions; discount the usual tautologies and clichés praising or condemning money, and it soon becomes apparent that the common knowledge of money consists of notions and conjectures the vagueness of which is astonishing compared with the relative precision of answers to questions about the movements of the moon, the stars, the atom, or the technicalities of launching a satellite.

The sad truth is that most people have a better understanding of the mechanics of the solar system than of the nature of money. People are generally aware that the earth is one of a number of planets which gravitate around the sun, which is one of many stars in a galaxy, and so on; they are also aware that matter is made up of atoms, which, when manipulated in certain ways, can have various interesting side effects. But few have any idea of how money circulates, of what makes it so useful and volatile. Yet it is money, not space travel or particle physics, that each of us is expected to make dozens of decisions about every day. To put it bluntly, what happens in the meetings of the governors of the Federal Reserve Bank, on the commodities markets, or in the foreign-exchange trading rooms of the major banks has a far more direct impact on our daily lives than the rings of Saturn or, nuclear war or power reactor meltdowns excepted, atomic theory. The ignorance is so complete that it seems accepted wisdom that only the chairman of the Federal Reserve Board understands anything about the process of "creating money."

Money Specialists to the Rescue

This confusion and ignorance has favored the emergence of a variety of experts and specialists, ranging from the disinterested scholar to the swindling charlatan, all of whom claim some insight into the "money world." Confronted with this seemingly incomprehensible universe, most people either give up trying to understand anything about the complexities of money and are satisfied to let these experts argue and sort things out among themselves, or they hire money specialists to provide them with interpretations, predictions, explanations, and guidelines. Both attitudes amount to an acknowledgment of the superiority of the experts' money savvy, the first option being more typical of the poor, the second one more characteristic of the rich, who seem so baffled by money that they retain the services of legions of accountants, financial planners, and investment counselors to keep abreast of the trends of the "money world."

The Experts at Work

The most visible part of the experts' activity is the booming, highly profitable and relatively risk-free industry of money commentary. Today's fastest-growing magazines are about making money, a dramatic switch from a few years ago, when sex, drugs, rock 'n' roll, and psychology were the hot topics. Every news show, every talk show, every newspaper, not merely in the big cities but also in the backwoods, has at least one money commentator on retainer, either directly or through syndication. Apart from such industry stalwarts as *Fortune, The Wall Street Journal,* and *Business Week,* the reader has a wide choice of sources, from obscure tip sheets to expensive newsletters to mass-circulation money glossies like *Money* magazine or *Inc.* More recently, radio and television have been devoting ever-increasing amounts of their precious airtime to the dissection of "money issues." *The Wall Street Journal* has become the most trusted and widely read daily newspaper in America because it acknowledges the importance of money and makes a good show of scrutinizing world events from what seems to be a money-smart perspective. People may watch the *MacNeil-Lehrer News Hour,* the *CBS Evening News,* or Ted Koppel's *Nightline* to get the headlines, but when it comes to understanding the issues, they rely more and more on such shows as *Wall Street Week* and *Adam Smith's Money World.*

The money literature offers various more advanced levels of money commentary. Best-selling books such as

those by Andrew Tobias, Sylvia Porter, and "Adam Smith,"
along with the endless string of biographies devoted to
the likes of Howard Hughes and J. Paul Getty, offer a
degree of insight beyond the entry-level expertise found
in the business section of newspapers or the "your money"
segment of radio and television newscasts. Unfortunately,
too many of these publications merely supply pop money
lore for the masses, simply catering to the public's fascination with intrigue by reducing money to a conspiracy
theory, either by elaborating the conspiracy theory (some
variation on "how the rich got rich by screwing you") or
by promising to make the reader privy to the conspiracy
itself ("how you, too, can become rich by screwing others").

Another sizable chunk of the pop money literature consists of the many money how-to books. This money gossip
includes supposedly hot tips and ideas which have made
some people rich but which do not work anymore, as
well as moral platitudes of the *Poor Richard's Almanac*
variety (things like "It takes money to make money," or
"You can make money without money if you really believe in yourself," or "Robots can make an automobile,
but they will never buy one"). The promise, open or tacit,
is the sharing of "inside information" with the reader.
But even the more accurate and sophisticated "insider's
reports" and investment tip sheets never carry the really
lucrative, truly "inside" information of the kind that makes
fortunes and attracts the attention of such regulators as
the Securities and Exchange Commission.

No matter how dogmatic and unrealistic their advice,
no matter how erroneous their trend-spotting analyses,
the myriad money-oriented TV and radio programs, investment newsletters, money scholars, and political economy ideologues somehow manage to keep pontificating
in their own way to their own committed, satisfied, and
faithful following. This audience keeps showing respect,
gratefulness, and appreciation even when its money gurus are proven wrong. The reason for this is that the
experts' mistakes are probably as useful as their successes. Their mistaken or misleading analyses and predictions and the publicity that surrounds such blunders

(as when Milton Friedman predicted a recession, which never happened, for some time in 1984) have a highly therapeutic effect and tend to give a welcome boost to the layperson's ego: the individual may not exactly feel that he has outsmarted the experts, but he can draw some satisfaction from thinking that the experts are not really that much smarter than he is, despite all their scholarly knowledge and inside information.

Corporations and most very rich individuals are acutely aware of the shortcomings and biases of specialists' advice about money. So they hedge their bets by having every manner of specialist, chartist, analyst, and forecaster on retainer. This allows them, for instance, to balance the opinions of outside consultants against those provided by their in-house economists and trend watchers or against their top executives' hunches and to come up with a not-too-disastrous balance of not-too-wrong predictions and not-too-painful quick fixes with plenty of escape hatches. The experts do not object to this practice because it makes it more difficult for their employer or client to blame any single one of them for disastrous advice, and in the end it means that more money gets paid out to the profession as a whole.

The Experts Under Fire

Despite the uncanny ability of money experts as a whole to gloss over, or at least to recover from, their mistakes, one brand of experts, the economists, have been singled out as the all-purpose scapegoat of the modern intellectual political and business world. It is quite fashionable, especially (but not exclusively) in government circles, to bad-mouth economists, playing up to the general public's instinctive distrust of these, the most theoretically inclined of the money specialists. Ronald Reagan and Johnny Carson have been ridiculing economists for years. The "assume a can opener" joke about economists has been circulating for at least six or seven years, to the best of our recollection. (For those who haven't heard it yet: A number of variously skilled specialists, and an economist among them, are stranded on a desert island with only a can of beans and no tools to open it; they all come up with their own highly technical and highly impractical idea of how to open it, until the economist solves the problem by saying, "Assume a can opener.") To understand the present disrepute in which economists seem to be, one must trace its roots to the now-forgotten days of the Carter White House.

Lester Thurow has described the Carter presidency as "the age of economic imperialism," noting that "five of the sixteen Cabinet members had Ph.D.s in economics, with only four being the lawyers who normally occupy the corridors of power."[2] The reason for this is that politicians desperately needed some credible spokespersons and policy advocates, and at that point in time only the money experts could command any respect and get the public's ear: those were the years when the economy appeared to be falling apart, when the world was just getting used to floating exchange rates, and when massive political corruption and mishandling of the successive "oil shocks" and of the beginning of the twilight of the traditional, "smokestack" industries ruled out any possibility of a politically based social consensus. Of course, it did not strike too many people at the time that these disasters were themselves due to previous policymakers having followed the course charted for them by their economic advisers.

Nevertheless, during the age of economics, it seemed that no politician dared issue a public statement on any subject without having his speeches reviewed by at least one economist. When the bubble burst, the economists were therefore the perfect scapegoats for the latest costly series of politico-economic blunders which begat the Third-World debt crisis, the Synfuels and Arctic Oil fiascoes, the much publicized problems of the American farmers, and the various scandals and near scandals of the "other people's money" variety. As of this writing, the only economist left in the Reagan cabinet is George Schultz and he's secretary of state, a function quite removed from immediate economic decision-making. Even the former secretary of the treasury, Donald Regan, is an outspoken critic of economists ("I've been called bad names before— but economist?"), a man who came straight from the wheeling and dealing end of Wall Street, with no formal economic training. During that period it was generally acknowledged that Paul Volcker was the only bona fide economist to hold so-called major league power in Washington.

The economists' downfall was to a large extent orchestrated by politicians intent on getting back at these experts who had stolen the spotlight from them. Economists helped give an entire generation of discredited politicians a new lease on public life, supplying them with ideas and providing them with a kind of good-money-sense seal of approval. They performed their duty so well that they soon found themselves standing in the way of the return to prominence of the professional politicians and their born-again army of slogan coiners, speech writers, and think-tankers. The ideologues' simplifications were more appealing politically than the economists' generalities and nuanced statements. Now that political fundamentalism has somehow produced a politically engineered economic recovery which flies in the face not only of economic theory but of the simplest accounting principles [as David Stockman testifys], politicians are as keen on proclaiming the incompetence of economists as they were on invoking their dictums a few years ago; they heap scorn on the economists because they want the economists' fall from public grace to be at least as painful as their own was in the days of Watergate, double-digit inflation, and the Iranian hostage crisis.

The Experts Politicized

Now that politicians have managed once again to occupy the high ground, it should come as no surprise that the economists who get the most airplay and column space are those who are the most partisan and ideological; their biased and stilted interpretations of the money world generally serve to boost the credibility of pathetic political fundamentalists or fan the political hopes of proponents of a revival of "industrial policy" or of advocates of monetary reform. More and more, institutions like the Council of Economic Advisers tend to be populated by ideologues. The Reagan administration has pushed things one step further, creating an even more ideological stable of economists than the CEA, something called the President's Economic Policy Advisory Board, composed of people like Arthur B. Laffer, the curve-on-the-napkin man.

As the typical politician's bid for power is more and more often based on a platform of taming the money monster, claiming greater expertise in money matters than the experts themselves, or at the very least an expertise better than that of the opposition's experts, the political discourse on the economy will increasingly become a hodgepodge: a random walk through the woods of money theory, featuring supply-siders one week, monetarists the next, with cameo appearances by rational-expectationists, and proponents of "industrial policy" on the back burner, just in case.

More distressing and ominous is that appointments to the Federal Reserve Board itself tend to be interpreted according to the ideological background of the appointees, as in this *Wall Street Journal* editorial examining recent appointments to the Fed: "The real significance of the appointment of Manuel H. Johnson and Wayne Angell to the Federal Reserve Board was that neither is a monetarist. Mr. Johnson, indeed, is the first governor with not only some supply-side instinct but the complete model in his head."[3]

The Two Worlds of Money

Beyond the economists' woes and uncertainties, and beyond the disagreements and quibbles over what is and is not economically sound, it is no secret that money theory in general (not only economics but the related disciplines, like management and business administration) is out of joint with the reality of money. This theory is not even in tune with the most visible, accessible, and simple moneymaking activity, business. Business people, especially small-business people, who operate at the "micro" end of the economy, routinely complain that there is little of practical use in economic and business theory. Employers regularly deplore the trouble which business school graduates experience when the time comes for them to function in the typical business environment. Successful stockbrokers have nothing but scorn for the theories of academic or journalistic market watchers or the investment strategies of most highly schooled money managers. Pointing out the shortcomings of the money experts has even become a profitable sideline for such heavyweight economists as Lester Thurow (most notably in his book *Dangerous Currents: The State of Economics*) and economics Nobel Prize winner Wassily Leontieff.[4]

There are such discrepancies between money as described by the experts and money as experienced by ordinary people that it is as though there were two parallel and disconnected worlds of money, the world of day-to-day money and that of the money experts. Reading textbooks, treatises, and essays about money or business or listening to money specialists requires a dramatic suspension of disbelief. First, you must forget everything you have learned from your daily encounters with money, since the experts systematically discount this firsthand experience, starting with the universal fascination with money. Compared with the world of real, no-nonsense, day-to-day money, the experts' world looks like a strange affair. Its central element is still money, but the experts' brand of money bathes in a kind of antiseptic irreality.

Nowhere does the theory of money give more than a passing nod to the excitement which money generates in the real world. Instead, money phenomena are described in an esoteric jargon. As *The Economist* had to admit in its 1983 survey of the world's economy, "Money may talk, but its technical vocabulary is sometimes ambiguous." The ambiguity can be found in the vast array of money euphemisms which make up the money theorists' basic English, terms like "negative returns," "nonperforming assets," "disinflation," "cost of living," "comparative advantage," or "natural rate of unemployment."

All in all, money experts and forecasters are probably no more incompetent now than they were at the turn of the century. Their shortcomings are simply more obvious because the public and the money environment are more sophisticated and less forgiving than before. More and more people are demanding that the specialists come up with intelligent answers. The growing dissatisfaction with the money experts' discourse is not due to their erroneous forecasts or to their questionable methodologies; rather, it is traceable to the growing visibility of the dissociation between the specialists' assumptions about money on the one hand and the reality of money as it is experienced by the general public on the other. The public's gut reaction is to judge the experts not on the grounds of their contributions to science, but on the relevance of expert advice to their own lives: people tend to take a dim view, for instance, of the monetarists' appeals for a slow, steady growth of the money supply when they do not have enough money in their pockets to pay the mortgage.

Unable to come up with the money equivalent of the theory of relativity, the money specialists make their daily bread out of money relativism. "A theory a day keeps your critics at bay" seems to be the watchword and the key to the money expert's survival. The main reason for this sorry state of affairs is not the errors in predictions, the self-interest of the protagonists in the debate, or the lack of sufficient data or proper mathematical equations; the problem with today's money expertise is that the experts do not talk of real money. Instead, their reference point is an abstraction, "the economy." When ordinary people talk about the economy, what they are really talking about is how other people's money relates to or affects their own. The whole analysis/commentary show is totally foreign to the man in the street's perception of money, which is precisely the starting point of "economic behavior."

The Experts' Consensus on the Nature of Money

Of course, different money specialists offer different definitions of money, but the vitality and power of everyday money is remarkably absent from all of them. Some insist on money's role as the universal commodity, others on its usefulness as a store of value; some see money as "a tool, a means of measurement"; some stress the inherent neutrality of money, while others emphasize its effectiveness as a tool of government policy. Yet, diverse as the experts' definitions of money may seem, they nevertheless represent a consensus. The party line is that money is different things for different folks; money may well be everywhere, yet it is not essential; it could as well be shells, gems, or some other symbol of value. When all is said and done, the emphasis is always on money as a complex but generally predictable economic variable which moves within certain well-defined parameters; besides, in the last analysis, money belongs to the narrow sphere of payments. What matters is the "real economy," the world of raw materials, production, and distribution, not the "symbol economy" of money.

The vast majority of money experts agree with Peter Drucker that "we . . . know quite a bit about the factors and forces which encourage both greater productivity and greater capital formation. None of them, it should be said, is a factor of the 'symbol economy' of money and credit."[5] For example, the Canadian historian Jane Jacobs, who claims some money expertise, since her book is titled *Cities and the Wealth of Nations*, describes money as "a factor in depressing or stimulating production."[6] This is typical of contemporary money expertise. Actually, what we see here is a pure throwback to the great tradition of John Law and the American populists for whom money is simply a stimulant for trade (therefore, for them, cheap money was of the essence). For George Gilder, money consists of liabilities or debts, while John Kenneth Galbraith in his later years has come to insist on money's role as a rather ignoble instrument for the exercise of power, along with physical brutality, strong personalities, and the like. For Adam Smith the second, "money is useless except that people give it value."[7] Other scholars have stressed the role of money as a tool of macroeconomic policy, and for many of them who adhere to a kind of materialistic version of "In God We Trust," the only real money consists of balances at the Federal Reserve. For others, money is the stuff of which "rational expectations" are made. In another vein, some economists, along with Keynes, maintain that the majority of people live under a "money illusion"; that is, they imagine that what matters is the magnitude of the amount which appears on their paychecks, not what buying power they have. And most of us have probably heard, in one form or another, Norman Podhoretz's opinion that money is the dirty little secret of American life.[8]

Seen in perspective, acclaimed milestones in the theory of money, Keynesianism for instance, appear as minor alterations in viewpoint, timid readjustments in response to cataclysmic market failures (in Keynes's case, the aftermath of World War I and the Great Depression). Keynes's *General Theory of Money* was anything but a theory of money; like his monetarist successors, he never discusses money in any context other than the process of financing government activity and stimulating business. The overriding concern of Keynesians is shared by their monetarist critics: the drafting of ready-made guidelines on how to run a government and keep the nation's book-keeping tidy at the same time. Keynes's work is essentially a theory of finance which leaves unchallenged the basic money assumption of his predecessors.

Monetarists present themselves as the true champions of money among the experts, yet their basic notion of money is the most conventional. Their view, as summed up by Sir Alan Waters, is that money is just like any other commodity:

> The more plentiful the supply, the lower the price. This is the law that man ignores at his peril. Money, whether a commodity or paper token, is no exception. The larger the money supply, the lower the value of money and the higher the general level of prices. So fundamental. So obvious. Yet so neglected.[9]

As can be gathered from these words from one of the world's most influential monetarists, the sad truth is that monetarists have nothing new to say about money. Their center of interest is not money but the government; their main concern is the old Keynesian question of how money can most effectively be used as a means of social engineering. As Peter Drucker said of Milton Friedman, "His economics is nothing more than macroeconomics, with the national government as the one unit, the one dynamic force, controlling the economy through the money supply."[10] Monetarists, with their credo of "slow, steady monetary growth," are actually suggesting a legislated limit to the growth of money. For them nothing can be worse than "too much money," and as any fire-and-brimstone preachers, they have their version of hell and damnation to threaten the nonbelievers with: inflation. The underlying assumption is that people cannot be trusted with money; this is a view which the monetarists, who politically are archconservatives, share with their sworn enemies, the Russians, who have always had strict controls over currency and all other aspects of money.

The authors of textbooks are another interesting breed. In the latest revision of his classic textbook, Paul Samuelson acknowledges the importance of money ("Money definitely matters"[11]) but mainly in order to integrate the monetarist doctrine into his own overview of economics. Unlike ordinary people whose universe is expanded by money, people like Samuelson expand their intellectual universe so as to include diverging interpretations of money, but without questioning any of the basic assumptions about the nature of money: Samuelson may as well have said, "Monetarism definitely matters," an undeniable statement when one looks at the very real social and economic messes which inevitably happen when politicians like Augusto Pinochet or Margaret Thatcher try to implement the theories of Milton Friedman.

For the money pundits, money remains a sideshow to some main event called "the economy" or "the society." Little seems to have changed in their discourse since the time when no less an economic authority than Walter Bagehot (editor of the British journal *The Economist* in its most influential period in the nineteenth century, and author of such classics as *Universal Money* and *Lombard Street*) wrote that "the use of money is a fact of no importance for economic theory."[12] Mind you, Bagehot was in good company. Adam Smith (the first) saw money as an arbitrarily chosen store of value, like beads or shells; for him, the source of "true prices, as well as real wealth" is labor.[13] For Marx (more specifically, for the young Marx), money was a sleazy tool for the extraction of surplus value. The more contemporary money experts still share the same basic outlooks; it is as though the entire edifice of modern money expertise, against the evidence of real life, rested on John Stuart Mill's remark that money "only exerts a distinct and independent influence of its own when it gets out of order," but with a new twist: money only matters for the experts when it poses problems for the prevailing theories of money.

Microeconomics: The Creationist View of Money

The intellectual foundation of all money expertise, from small-business bookkeepers to macroeconomic forecasters, is microeconomics, the study of which invariably starts with the "man on the island" allegory, a rehashing of the adventures of Robinson Crusoe. The fictional description of the man on an island and how he organizes his environment is supposed to show the most basic economy of all. It is taught to every student of business, economics, and management in the entry-level course. Of course, there is no money on the hypothetical desert island. The underlying message is that, since the island has an "economy" but no money, money is not vital, that money has appeared more or less by chance, long after "the economy" was in operation. There have also been some more modern examples of a basic economy, the most pernicious of which is probably the use of the concentration camp as an example of a basic economy.[14] Here, the prisoners are shown to be economic agents: some save their rations, later to trade them at a premium with others who are not so farsighted. The result is the same as that of the desert island tale: money is not an essential feature of economic life. The theorists who use these analogies invariably show that "the economy" is everywhere, from time immemorial: in prehistoric times, in ancient Rome, in feudal and medieval societies, and in what they usually describe as "the modern market economy." In this context, the specificity of our times, the paramount importance of money, becomes little more than a sideshow.

Because of the disregard for money's central role in the economic process, the tenets of money expertise are reminiscent of the religious theory of creationism, which holds that man somehow appeared on earth, out of nowhere, as a kind of afterthought to creation, because God somehow felt like it. For economists, money is an afterthought to the economy; it somehow appeared because man felt like it.

From a Theory of Abundance to the Management of Scarcity

The main concerns of the first economists, generally known as the classical economists, people like Adam Smith and John Stuart Mill, were wealth and its growth. Over the years, mostly because of the widespread acceptance of the pessimistic prognostications of Thomas Malthus and his followers, economics became a codification of set principles about the management of scarcity. Economic expertise as we know it is not focused on money—that is, on wealth and abundance—but on unemployment and politics, the management of the labor market, and the allocation of resources, which are defined as inherently limited. We are constantly reminded by all sorts of pundits that the term "economics" is derived from the Greek word meaning "household" or some such thing, "economy" being the efficient running of one's household, a rather simple exercise in the management of scarcity.

This is perhaps the most fundamental difference between the everyday world of money and that of the experts. The experts' world is dominated by the notion of scarcity, while for most people money holds the promise of plenty. Experts invariably present money as an economic instrument, a management tool, something to administer the scarcity of resources with. But in the real world, money means abundance, not scarcity, as in "to be in the money."

Money not only implies wealth in the present for some individuals; it is also mankind's prime instrument to deal with time, the ultimate constraint. Money does not only carry the notion of plenty in the here and now; it offers the perspective of plenty of time. The commonplace "time is money" is perhaps the most basic recognition of this. Money is mankind's collective bid against time, the privileged medium which can make possible the realization of dreams in spite of the relentless passage of time. Already, some modern dynasties, like the Vanderbilts and the Rockefellers, have lasted longer than many dynasties of legend; their strength is that they are based on money, not on the exercise of power or military exploits; power usually starts to disintegrate as soon as the founder of a dynasty or the builder of an empire dies, while money makes it possible for wealth to remain and even grow long after its original creator is gone.

When Worlds Collide

What we are left with is a severe dissociation between the theory of money and the reality of money. This dissociation leads to some inevitable clashes between an inadequate, scarcity-centered theory and an ever-changing, ever-richer, reality. Our limited understanding of money, the central element of our lives, produces the kind of appalling results which make up a good share of the headlines.

Like galaxies, the two worlds of money seldom intersect, but when they do, catastrophes happen because theories are implemented which *a priori* exclude real-world money, which returns to haunt the implementers in the form of massive unforeseen side effects. In recent years monetarists of strict obedience (described by Lester Thurow as "A-bomb monetarists"[15]) have convinced various governments to go ahead with what James Tobin described as "the single minded anti-inflation crusades" that dominated the world economic scene of the early 1980s: "The crusades certainly succeeded in breaking the back of inflation," adds Tobin, "but at great costs in production, employment and investment, costs that have scarely abated in most of the Organization for Economic Co-operation and Development [OECD] countries outside of North America."[16] Bank runs are a good example of the two worlds intersecting: depositors insist on seeing whatever they consider as "real money" while the banks' and the government's experts keep talking about transfers of funds, deposit insurance, and the stability of the banking system. The specter of a more frightening cataclysm along these lines was raised by John Kenneth Galbraith: the possibility that the unthinkable, a run on the dollar by foreign investors, may happen because of the kind of financial politics which have been implemented in recent years at the urge of some trusted and presumably competent money specialists.[17]

Less spectacular but equally significant are the tragedies, public and private, which happen when, for example, lending institutions, adhering to a kind of accountant's definition of money, conclude that the more loans they have on the books, the richer, hence the more successful, the bank is. Inevitably they become involved with consumers, small-business people, and farmers, whose views of money are as naive as theirs. These in turn assume that if a bank will loan them money, they must be doing something right. One false notion about money (the bank's) leads to another (the borrowers) and ultimately to a whole integrated system of punishment without rehabilitation involving the pitiful world of credit bureau investigations, auditors, bailiffs, repossession specialists, and debtor's court. All of this leading to the fantastic conclusion that money is heartless and amoral.

Toward Money Literacy: Beyond Scarcity Thinking

It is the man-in-the-street kind of money which moves things, which starts and stops those movements which, quite a long time after the fact, become statistically documented and officially branded as recessions, recoveries, expansions, depressions, inflations, and "stagflations." Far from having their finger on the pulse of the money trends, the money experts are more like the astronomers who, because of the distances involved and the finite speed of light, observe stars which have already disappeared. For instance, it took until August 1974 for the National Bureau of Economic Research to diagnose officially the recession which had started in November of 1973 and which was already very sorely felt at every level of society.[18] Some experts, dissatisfied with the various "leading indicators," have even come to the conclusion that one of the best economic "barometers" is "a little-known composite index ... appropriately called the index of lagging indicators."[19] In other words, our understanding of money is so imperfect that the most solid expertise is that which comes after the fact. What constantly derails the experts' forecasts is precisely that the real world does not abide by their limited definitions of money; since people are constantly finding new ways of making money and new dimensions to money, they regularly short-circuit all the policies and plans elaborated by the money specialists.

We are stuck in a kind of chicken-and-egg routine: the experts try to understand the behavior of people toward money, while these people look to the experts for advice about what to do with their money. The way out would be to disentangle our thinking from the specialists' abstractions, to realize that what we take with us whenever we leave the house—money—does not represent some kind of alien force which burns holes in our pockets and which elicits scarcity-oriented, "economic" behavior. Money in the modern sense of the word represents both the possibility of wealth and the way to obtain that wealth; money opens countless roads to riches; it is not a limited and limiting set of options.

The problem with the prevailing money expertise is not, as has so often been presented in the editorial pages of newspapers and business magazines, that the experts do not take all the economic variables into account, or that they fail to assess the political climate accurately. The underlying problem of all the "crises in economic theory" in particular and of the more general malaise surrounding our understanding of money processes is that money itself and the attitudes of ordinary people toward money are left out of the picture altogether, sooner or later calling attention to themselves, usually by derailing the best-laid economic and business plans and forecasts, sometimes at frightening cost. The approach to such vitally important public issues as world hunger, the control of inflation and public indebtedness, and the distribution of wealth can only be brought back on the right track if we make a drastic switch away from considering people as having an "economic behavior" and toward concentrating on their relationship to money. We can no longer afford to be guided by a theory of scarcity because we live in a world whose essential force—money—is the very opposite of scarcity. Money is essentially social, not antisocial; money does not force us to accept limits and to adapt our behavior to patterns sanctioned by specialists; on the contrary, money offers the possibility of overcoming limits and restraints.

───── Money Myth 2: ─────

Like Death and Taxes, Money Is One of Life's Constants

THE MYTH: Money today is the same as it has been for thousands of years. It obeys the same laws, even though its physical form may have altered from the original precious metal, and it elicits the same questionable behavior, namely greed and selfishness, in seemingly decent people as it always has. The corollary is that, since money is eternal and its influence on humans immutable, there are eternal laws governing the management of money and a narrow range of options for running a money-based society.

The Myth in Action

Money is seen as an entity which remains the same through time and space. This gives rise to the presumption that there is a common fund of money wisdom which has applied and will apply to all forms of money. And since money never changes, it is assumed that the reasons for wanting money never change, either. The passion that people feel for money is at best suspect because this enthusiasm is presumed to be based on those attitudes which common wisdom ascribes to perennial money: selfishness and greed.

The message is that the men and women of the 1980s are dealing with the same money in the same way as their forebears, the ancient prophets or the characters in a Shakespeare play. When an entire generation makes money its priority, its elders portray it as pursuing the same old money they did, as perpetuating the tradition of acquisitiveness and work ethic. This is reminiscent of the oversimplifications of pop psychology which portray contemporary individuals as struggling with the exact same neuroses and anxieties which are believed to have affected Freud's patients in early-twentieth-century Vienna, or some mythical ancient Greeks like Oedipus.

When money is turned into something more or less eternal, it is relegated to the level of death and taxes, these other immutable constraints acknowledged by popular wisdom; instead of being recognized as a privileged effector of change and a source of unending excitement, money is perceived as a burden, an impediment, as something to be conquered, overcome.

Eternal Money

The idea that money never changes is deeply rooted in both popular and "high" culture as well as in the tenets of money expertise. Poets, theologians, and moralists all seem to agree with the money experts on at least one item of money lore: the timelessness of money. Of course, these intellectuals look at money from their particular, more or less esoteric, fanatic or eclectic vantage point, but the various descriptions of money which they offer all have a touch of the eternal about them.

For centuries, poets have either reviled money as the constant perverter of human relationships or, more sensibly, heaped abstract praise on it. Religion's notion of money has not changed much since Saint Paul warned his disciple Timothy (1 Timothy 6:10) of the love of money being the root of all evil. To this day, this is the party line dutifully adhered to by such theological luminaries as the Pope, the Ayatollah Ruhollah Khomeini, and the Dalai Lama. Even patently money-oriented evangelists such as the Reverend Sun Yung Moon do not depart noticeably from this orthodoxy, at least in their preachings.

Moralistic social commentators have also done their fair share to describe money as an immutable entity, often presenting it as an ignoble tool for the exercise of power, as an instrument of oppression and social control. Money is most often cast in the role of the great corruptor and all-purpose social malefactor. Pacifists, for example, routinely insist that money has been from time immemorial the cause of all wars.

Of course, there are positive variants on these themes; the book of Ecclesiastes says (10:19), "Money answereth all things"; Francis Bacon is on the record as opposing the conventional notion that money is the sinews of war, and George Bernard Shaw in his play *Major Barbara* stresses the civilizing role of money: "The universal regard for money is the one hopeful fact of our civilization, the one sound spot in our social conscience. Money is the most important thing in the world. It represents health, strength, honour, generosity and beauty. . . ." But even those positive views of money imply that it is impervious to change, that it remains constant through space and time. Answer to all things, universal commodity, great corrupter, instrument of power, warmonger, or eighth wonder of the world: no matter what alleged trait of money a particular definition stresses, the implication is that money has always been, and always will be, endowed with this or that characteristic.

This notion of money as a constant of life through time and space is firmly rooted in the classic references to money which abound in mythology, chronicles, and legends, from the early tales about the Golden Calf, Midas, and Croesus, through the *Rheingold* saga. Closer to us, the prospectors in *The Treasure of the Sierra Madre* end up being killed by their lust for money; in *Goldfinger* James Bond is confronted with a ruthless megalomaniac driven by greed. This tradition presents money as a permanent fixture of our lives, an entity unaffected by historical development, a kind of curse that has been with us at least since the beginning of recorded history. According to this great tradition, money, generally in the form of gold, keeps on eliciting the same Pavlovian responses in humans rich and poor, primitive and civilized: ruthlessness, selfishness, and murderous instincts are seen as permanently and inextricably intertwined with money (and vice versa).

Timeless money, whether it appears under the guise of bullion, coins, paper notes, or securities, is the perennial troublemaker. Ever since Balzac and Dickens, drama and literature have been portraying people confronted with troubles brought about by money or the lack of it. Money is invariably cast as the catalyst for lust, homicidal scheming, pathological jealousy, and sundry criminal and repugnant behavior, most notably in detective fiction, for instance in such classics as *Double Indemnity*, *Dial M for Murder*, and *Strangers on a Train*, where money pushes relatively normal, if flawed, characters to commit murder. Hammett's elusive Maltese Falcon is nothing but eternal money pushing people to lie and betray their lovers and friends.

The ruthless, greedy, and despicable money-driven individual is also a staple of more pedestrian attempts at dramatization, such as television's *Dallas* and *Dynasty*. The vast majority of modern dramatic creations depict how more and more people are experiencing money-related and money-induced trouble, not because money has changed, but simply because there is more money in more hands than ever before, with the result that more people have come under its influence and consequently experience money troubles. Money as portrayed even in the most contemporary literature, drama, and cinema is not that much different from the money of Scrooge or Shylock; what is new is the multitude and magnitude of the money-related problems in a world centered on money. It is as though contemporary life, dominated as it is by money, were a nightmarish sequel to Wagner's *Ring*: after the twilight of the gods, the gold has not been returned to the Rhinemaidens, and it is wreaking havoc among the mortals; the woes inflicted by money, once an exclusive nightmare of the mighty few, are now the lot of the common man. This seems a very pernicious message, a sort of perverted preaching in praise of poverty and privilege, a way of saying that things were a lot better for the common folks when only the rich had money.

Affirmations of the unvarying nature of money are not very different from the opinion widely held by money experts that money is simply carrying out the functions which have been fulfilled from time immemorial by beads, shells, and bullion; the timelessness of money is at the root of the notion that money is simply the modern embodiment of some kind of universal commodity, a means of payment or a store of value.

More fundamentally, there lurks behind all this a profoundly pessimistic message about the immutability of human nature. The depiction of money as unaffected by the passage of time serves to prop up theories such as biological determinism which posit the eternal selfishness of mankind and its propensity to endlessly repeat past mistakes. And here again, the classic value judgments about money are only reinforced by expert opinion, and vice versa. The deterministic, pessimistic world view is well served by the classic economic concept of *Homo economicus*, a kind of contrived, lopsided character exclusively responsive to, indeed totally obsessed with, his selfish interests, who abides by some kind of genetically transmitted code of money etiquette based on ancestral greed.

The Myth Unraveled: Money Changes Everything, and Nothing Changes More Than Money Itself

There is a major problem with this view of money as the eternal, ubiquitous, and invariable mover of events involving humans whose neuroses, reflexes, and behavior never change: it simply does not conform to either the historical or the contemporary reality of money. Human nature may or may not change; but money is constantly changing and precipitating change. Even a casual study of everyday conversation reveals that we are right in the middle of momentous changes affecting our perception of money, changes which have yet to be reflected in literature and philosophy. Moreover, a close look at some well-known contemporary events and phenomena shows how these perceptual changes are indicative of significant changes in money itself which have barely been hinted at either by economic theory or by the more common cultural references to money.

Money Was Not Always Taken for Granted

Money is now so firmly established as the quintessentially modern way of doing things that it is hard to imagine a different state of affairs. But it is important to realize that the generalization of money is a recent phenomenon. Most of our parents have some recollection of moneyless transactions as an everyday occurrence. Even as late as the 1960s, money was far from taken for granted; in fact, the "Fabulous Sixties," even though they were a time of opulence, were also years of intense intellectual and moral reaction against money. The 1960s' counter-cultural movement was the last great romantic rejection of money. Of course, this has given way to today's general awareness that there is no viable alternative to a money-based society. But the further one looks in the past, the less accepted money appears to have been.

The social reformers of the nineteenth century are generally considered to be utopians because of their visions of a world without money. In fact, they did not have to look very far for their model. At the time, a world without money was not a romantic ideal. It was not only conceivable, it was a painful reality. The nineteenth century was characterized by the uneasy coexistence between money and the obsolescent, traditional systems of slavery and barter. Money was then only beginning to assume its modern, universal role; it had yet to be introduced on a large scale in most of Asia and Africa, not to mention vast sectors of the European agricultural areas (Russia, for instance). Even in America money was nowhere near dominance. Rather than being a series of "straight money deals," the drive westward depended to a large extent on outright land grabbing, while life in the South was based on slavery; in either case, there was a serious lack of money. The reality of the West was probably close to the image which most of us can remember of John Wayne, in the movie *Red River*, living on a ranch with ten thousand heads of cattle but having no money and faced with the formidable task of driving his cattle across the Red River to Kansas in order to sell them.

In this context it is quite understandable that, as late as 1870, one could conclude that the dissolution of the European monarchies and of the Russian autocracy might end up producing some kind of social bond other than money. Clearly, this did not happen except in places like Russia where money was in a state of severe underdevelopment to start with. Nineteenth-century visions of a world without money are more the result of a lack of imagination on the part of aspiring social reformers than a consequence of utopianism.

In every instance the various forms of totalitarianism in the twentieth century were directed against money. This is true of both fascism (Hitler was decidedly antimoney and only tolerated German industry to the extent that it followed his orders) and Stalinism (no money in the Kremlinology). In a recent and tragic instance, Cambodia's Khmer Rouge, for example, were such rabid antimoney romantics that they destroyed all the money in the country's central bank. All of these events were tragic and bloody reactions against money, but they should also be recognized as an expression of nostalgia for a time when money was not the dominant force. That this nostalgia exists at all is the most compelling reminder not only that money was not always taken for granted but also that we should never take it for granted, lest it be taken away from us, with dire consequences.

The Age of Money

The main characteristic of our times is that for the first time money is the sole preferred way of transacting business. Money has finally displaced the older system of barter. The statistical evidence is overwhelming: the violent culture shock brought about by the universality, the flexibility, and the volatility of money has by now reached every part of the world. The barter system evolved over centuries (indeed it still dominated world trade as recently as the turn of the century), but it has been rapidly displaced by money. Despite some headline-making estimates that barter makes up to 40 percent of world trade, there is much evidence to show that if one excludes barter among the Soviet bloc countries, then at most barter represents a scant 9 percent of world trade, and this figure includes barter between communist countries and the West. The conclusion is inescapable: Barter only survives as a viable way of transacting business when there are political or moral restrictions on money. One regularly encounters news items touting the rebirth of barter, but such occurrences are invariably related to the plight of multinational corporations which, stuck in the currency-controls and foreign-exchange quagmire, resort to countertrade (bartering one commodity for another and then selling the second for some hard currency) and other cumbersome maneuvers in order to circumvent political restrictions on the flow of money. "The moral is plain: barter flourishes when finance fails to oil the wheels of normal commercial trade."[1]

But there is more. Countertrade deals and barter arrangements are quite complicated, more complicated than straight money deals, because of the procedures, the delays, and the general inflexibility involved. "Enter, for that reason, the bankers and consultants and lawyers. There is a strong prima facie case that they are the biggest beneficiaries of the fad for countertrade."[2]

Money Through the Ages

No one knows exactly when or where money originated, and the issue is further confused because a number of historians and money experts insist that many things were used as money over the years. We feel comfortable with Galbraith's notion that "for all practical purposes, for most of time, money has been a more or less precious metal," and that "more awkward or exotic items such as cattle, shells, whiskey and stones, though greatly relished by teachers on money, have never been durably important for people much removed from primitive rural existence."[3] From the very beginning, money was fundamentally different from the "universal commodities," the shells, beads, and other means of exchange and stores of value of which it is supposedly an outgrowth. By simply looking at the current impact of money on the premoney cultures of Asia and Africa, one can imagine the same kind of clash between money and those primitive forms of exchange centuries ago. Money always has cataclysmic effects when introduced in remote areas; no sooner is it let loose than cultures and societies which have endured for centuries are turned upside down or choose to flee far away from the new way of doing things. This is fundamental: no ideology, no social standard, no substitute "universal commodity" ever had this kind of wide-ranging cultural impact. It is quite likely that there was never a slow, gradual evolution toward money. Rather, the emergence of money in a given society marked a dramatic rupture with the traditional way of life centered on slavery, barter, and tribalism.

Blows Against the Empire: The Fight Against Darkness

Apart from the coins which have survived, we know little about money in antiquity. But the evidence suggests that very early on, money was important to commerce and the social organization and that its emergence brought up some important questions which are still connected with money such as honesty and the role of the state toward money. According to Galbraith, instances of counterfeiting can be found as early as 540 B.C.[4]

But antiquity seems to have been characterized by a chronic shortage of money. The only money consisted of coins and precious metal, and these were always threatened with debasement whenever the current tyrant or emperor needed some petty cash; there was no fiduciary money whatsoever. Money was not lent, let alone credit advanced, for productive uses, but strictly to advance the ends of pure power. A large proportion of the upper classes' income certainly came from moneylending, but this essentially consisted of usurious, mostly short-term loans to the poor, not of investment in wealth-producing ventures. Rome was not exactly the land of money: members of the professions did not get paid; rather, they collected favors. Such was probably the foundation of the great Mafia tradition of favors owed and granted and of offers which cannot be safely refused.

Michael Harrington notes that "even in Greece and Rome, the most advanced of societies in ancient times, the full development of money appears only at the point of decadence and decline."[5] In our opinion this stresses the extent to which money was foreign to the ways of an empire built on foreign conquest, plunder, and slavery. Money, along with the emergence of Christianity, was one of the essential elements in the bringing down of an overbearing, outmoded imperial state based on slavery and outrageous use of military power.

Yet no matter how essentially contradictory the idea of

money and that of the empire were, a deal of sorts had been struck between money and the empire, as reported in the "render unto Caesar" episode of the Gospel. As a result, the currency of the Roman Empire was the only thing remotely resembling what we now call a monetary system in the Western world. Thus the fall of the empire translated into a painful setback for money. For all practical purposes, whatever monetary system Europe had disappeared with the fall of the empire. The Dark Ages were a sorry time of no money.

The Middle Ages were the golden age of the money myths: money and money-handlers condemned as evil, banking severely limited by church authorities, all-around scarcity of money. This period was dominated by the fierce raiding by feudal warlords of one another's bullion stashes. Plundering precious metal was the driving force of most medieval military expeditions, including the Crusades. At least half the incentive for the quest of the Holy Grail came from the Grail being made of precious metal, the stuff money was made of. Hoarding bullion was the goal of all medieval warlords and monarchs. In a tragic episode, the Order of the Knights Templars was dissolved and its members subjected to dreadful tortures because the Templars, having learned the trade from the Jews in Palestine, had become bankers, and their early adherence to the dynamics of money deprived kings and popes alike of the monies they needed to wage their private wars.

The Money Renaissance

The Renaissance was characterized by the rebirth of money. Even under its clumsy, precious-metal forms, money led the recovery of civilization. The search for money-related metals was the driving force behind the great expeditions which led to breakthroughs in our knowledge of the universe, including the discovery of America, much in the same way that the alchemists' quest for the philosophers' stone, the age-old dream of turning base metals into gold and silver—into money—was the guiding light of what was to become modern chemistry.

The insufficient supply of precious metals in Europe made for a scarcity of money. This basic scarcity in turn was stifling the expansion of trade and commerce. The great explorers' forays in the New World, most notably the voyages of Francis Drake, put an end to this, with some epochal consequences.

Needless to say, money was still inhibited by the inflexibility of its metallic form, but the sudden abundance of bullion soon opened up new perspectives, which were reflected by the unprecedented explosion in creativity and questioning of the established order which characterized the Italian as well as the English renaissances. The quantum leap in the money supply caused by the arrival in Europe of American gold rapidly created the need for a more versatile kind of money. The first major step toward this end was the introduction of paper money. Paper money first showed up as a stand-in for precious metal, which was becoming far too bulky to keep up with the ever-accelerating pace of trade and commerce. This is the kind of money which was central to the European renaissance and the end of the old feudal order:

> Keynes linked the flowering of European culture, literature, science, and the arts to the arrival of "the booty brought back by Drake in the *Golden Hind.*" ... One might note in passing that a leading Soviet political economist and authority on money, Stadnichenko, associates the disintegration of feudalism with the appearance of paper money in Europe, an event linked, of course, to the arrival of Drake's booty.[6]

Feudalism is often portrayed by nostalgics as a kind of benevolently paternalistic institution which was displaced by the faithless and heartless cohorts of money. Of course, the aim of this historical misrepresentation is to heap blame on money. Feudalism was based on the forced exchange of goods and services in return for military protection. Thanks to money, it became possible for goods and even for labor itself to be exchanged for money. With money one did not have to resort to the protection of the local warlord; money could buy whatever protection one felt was needed. Money even offered the option of moving to a more secure location, first to town and later to the "new world," for instance. Money ended the individual's subordination to a power structure determined by geography, heredity, or palace intrigues. The new relationships based on money were a radical departure from the previous relationships based on submission to some absolute authority. It has been said that the end of the feudal order marked the end of cyclical time, a worldview dominated by the eternal return of the seasons, of sowing and harvesting, of summer followed by winter; this was replaced by linear, historical time, where life acquires a meaning different from the endless repetition of the cycles of nature; seen in this light, the saying "Time is money" takes on a whole new meaning.

The supersession of bullion-based money by paper money was a major historical turning point, and like all innovations it took a long time to be fully understood, appreciated, and accepted as a normal fact of life. There was such a distrust of the new, "pure" kind of money that it was thought safer to keep it under control by tying the value of currency to a bullion-derived standard; the link between money and national gold reserves was severed only recently, after the stubborn adherence to the gold-standard gospel had created an almost catastrophic shortage of money. In fact, a surprising degree of confusion persists to this day in many a mind about the convertibility of the dollar, pound, escudo, yen, ruble, or franc notes into gold or silver, many people being firmly convinced that the paper they hold is not "real" money, that it owes its value to the stashes of bullion hidden away in the vaults of Fort Knox or of the Bank of England. Even more disquieting are the periodic appeals, which seem to come from every sector of the intellectual and political spectra, either for a return to the gold standard or for the "keying" of currencies to some external, nonmonetary reference point.

The move away from metallic money dealt a painful blow to an archetypal attitude toward money: the hoarding mentality. Besides being cumbersome and in limited supply, metallic money suffered from another drawback, hoardability. During the age of metal, wealth and hoarding had been inseparable. Up until the early twentieth century, the hoarding instinct and the quasireligious belief in bullion (as in "will pay the bearer on demand") were the main causes of the financial panics which periodically sent the world economy for nasty spins. The change from metallic money to credit money was an important step toward avoiding panic in the banking system.[7] Money is no longer a physical presence, something to be worshiped and fondled (gold bullion was very sexy indeed), lovingly weighed, and stored in strongboxes. Today's money tends to be essentially intangible, even for the wealthiest of us. The most "real" money is quite simply the movement of money; beholding bullion or hoarding precious metal or currency does not contribute to making money move; it is no way to treat money. The mythology about wealth, money, and the hoarding mentality may not have changed, but in the real world, money is definitely not conforming to it. Linking money and hoarding is like clinging to a children's notion of wealth: the one who has the greatest number of toys is the richest.

America, the Continent of Money

The history of America reads like the history of the changes that lead up to money as we know it, modern money. The discovery of the American continent, as we have already noted, was motivated in no small part by the quest for gold and silver, which at the time were the main forms of money. The precious metals which had, over centuries, been in every sense of the word immobilized in the Incan and Mayan temples and mortuaries were finally put to productive use when they were melted down and minted into the doubloons and sovereigns which were desperately needed to fuel the development of Europe.

The development of North America is even more intimately linked to money-related innovations, as we will see in some detail in a subsequent chapter. From the arrival of the Pilgrims, through the tax revolt which led to the independence of the colonies and the birth of the Republic, to the California Gold Rush, money was the unifying force in the developing American society. The American continent was being peopled by individuals and communities dissatisfied with the stultifying social and economic status quo of Europe. The unique kind of money practices which developed in the United States— the mainstay of which was America's unique, highly decentralized banking system—was the practical alternative to the petrified aristocratic, clerical, and bureaucratic social order of the Old World. Democratic access to money was at least a possibility for the first time.

The Twilight of the Money Liturgy: The Medium Is Not the Message

Only recently, people stood in awe of the outer trappings of money: a checking account was an important symbol of respectability, and a visit to the bank was a significant event for anyone, surrounded by expectations and decorum. Money itself was very much like a sacrament, residing in tabernacle-like strongboxes and vaults. How things have changed. Yesterday's fascination with the liturgy of money has given way to a tendency to treat money as an everyday thing, not as something exceptional, commanding a whole set of rituals. This change in how money is perceived is well illustrated by the ready acceptance by the public at large of the computer terminals and banking machines which are replacing snooty tellers and lavishly decorated bank halls, as well as putting an end to the nonsense of "bankers' hours," and which are even threatening to displace inquisitive loan officers. Clearly, what matters is money, not its technicalities.

The development of "electronic money" and the comments it has brought forth offer an interesting example of the changes which money is undergoing and of the widespread misinterpretation which can be made of them when observers focus on technicalities. Electronic money is money you cannot see or touch, although it has more fluidity and influence than ever. However, the general tendency is to credit technology, mostly the improvements in telecommunications, for the sweeping changes affecting the way money moves around the world. Even such an astute observer of the evolution of banking as Martin Mayer insists that much of the current evolution is due to the introduction of new technologies.[8] This is like saying that people talk to each other because they have a telephone; obviously, people don't talk to each other just because the telephone was invented; they do so because they have something to communicate. In the case of the worldwide money networks, it would be more accurate to say that technology is trying to keep up with the frantic pace of modern money: the whole world desperately needs ever greater amounts of money around the clock, so it has developed appropriate supply lines.

Technology alone cannot be substituted for modern money and modern attitudes toward money. The so-called smart card, a bank card with an embedded microchip memory, was developed in France; automated tellers were introduced in Europe earlier than in America; and Canada has had nationwide overnight check-clearing for years, something which still does not exist in the United States. Yet in all those countries, money is notoriously less "modern" than in the United States.

Toward Money Literacy: New Money, New Attitudes

Ours are fascinating times, a period when we can witness the emergence of a new money awareness concomitant with tremendous changes affecting all aspects of money, including attitudes toward saving and investing. In today's world, where money is more omnipresent, faster moving, and more volatile than ever, money is no longer seen as the dirty secret of private and public affairs, and even the stigma traditionally attached to bankruptcy is being questioned. All of this signals a welcome departure by large segments of public opinion from the classic notion that money never changes and that, therefore, our money habits should never depart from the inherited norm.

There Are No Rainy Days with Modern Money, and No Shelters Either

The pessimistic, money-moralistic legacy of the 1930s, "this can't last, better squirrel some of it away," is a thing of the past. No longer is money seen as something to be accumulated patiently and reserved as a protection against hard times. Smart money bets on the future, but it is increasingly futile to try and use money to hedge your bets *against* the future. Money may be your friend in need, but not unconditionally so: money will be good to you only if you treat it well. And today, treating your money well has little to do with the traditions of hoarding, penny-pinching, and "safe" investments. Modern money is the end of the line for such classic characters of money mythology as the coupon clipper; conventional money havens no longer offer the peaceful, no-surprise future they once did; the once ultra-secure utilities and municipal bonds markets are undergoing such modifications that a major bonds rater was recently quoted as

lamenting, "The whole world is going single-B," referring
to the fact that more and more bond issuers are losing
the superior ratings they used to have. There have been
such profound changes in the money markets that fluctu-
ations in interest rates which were simply unthinkable
ten years ago cause barely a shrug today. Interest rates
routinely change in a single week by as much as they
used to in a whole year, yet life goes on, and it goes on
mainly because what we are dealing with is a new kind of
money, which elicits new attitudes toward money. These
attitudes in turn go a long way toward explaining why
there are no generalized money-induced panics despite
the obviously serious financial and monetary problems of
recent years. The absence of massive bank runs and stock-
exchange collapses is usually ascribed to the experience
gained by central banks and regulating agencies, but in
fact the regulators and their powers have not changed
much since the Great Depression; what has changed,
however, is that people have realized that they are no
longer living with the same money as people in 1929.

The metaphor "safe as money in the bank" is a bit of
popular money wisdom which is rapidly being phased
out because of the ominous changes which money is undergoing. The growing feeling is that, unlike ten years
ago, the right place for money is anywhere but in the
bank, especially in these times when bank failures are
happening at what seems to be an ever-increasing rate,
and when money in the bank amounts, in the words of
Martin Mayer, to "little more than a government promise" to pay back something to the depositors in case there
is trouble. For many of the small depositors who were
stung in the recent rash of bank and near bank failures,
the most amazing realization was that even banks don't
keep their money in the bank. Banks, the archetypal
money institutions of yesteryear, are no longer perceived
as temples of money wisdom and prudence.

Bankruptcy Is No Longer a Social Disease

Under the old, vanishing code of money there were few stigmas more indelible than that attached to business failure or bankruptcy. Money had overtones of karma, and failure was bad money karma which stayed with you forever, like adultery, divorce, or an illegitimate child in a closely knit religious community; this was the perfect complement to the aura of mystery which surrounded the process by which businesses did or did not succeed. As money becomes increasingly user-friendly, it loses its aura of dispenser of reward and punishment for morally good behavior. The stigma traditionally attached to bankruptcy, for instance, is rapidly becoming a thing of the past, especially in the sectors of the economy which most depend on innovation and open-mindedness. It was especially so in the computer industry in its heyday. As *The Wall Street Journal* proclaimed in a front-page headline, "Silicon Valley loves a trail-blazer even if he does end up in bankruptcy court." As the article explains, "Almost anywhere else, a business failure taints a career, hurting relationships and hampering efforts to start anew. Here, though, perhaps the only dishonor is not to try again."[9] Anyone can measure the gulf which separates this attitude from the traditional view of money matters, as codified in such popular adages as "Neither a borrower nor a lender be."

The Changing Esthetics of Money: Money Is in the Eye of the Beholder

We are witnessing a remarkable change in the traditional relationship between art and money. Money has traditionally been used to acquire esthetically pleasing paintings, sculptures, or other works of art. This trend has now come full circle, as evidenced by the emergence of some "new financial instruments" that readily make it possible to use works of art as collateral for all kinds of loans. Nowadays, the main feature of a painting or a sculpture is most often its value in terms of money—that is, how much money the owner can borrow against it— much in the same way that financial success and profitable marketing are the overriding concerns of the new generation of artists and art gallery operators. The rise of Sotheby's to prominence among art auctioneers is due more to the recognition of art buyers' and sellers' financial needs than to a better feel of the artistic trends. There is every indication that we are about to see the end of the tradition of the immobilization, often for generations, of vast amounts of money in works of art; more and more, owners of valuable artworks will employ services like those offered by Sotheby's and use works of art as a financial tool. The trend is even affecting the usually staid art collectors of France and has caused business to boom at that two-century-old institution the Mont-de-Piété, which was founded in 1777 by Louis XVI as a kind of national pawnbroker to combat the usurers' outrageous interest rates, which could go as high as 10 percent a month. A nonpoor citizen recently borrowed, and promptly paid back, 150,000 francs at 17 percent against a Renoir for a stock-exchange operation.[10] As money changes and becomes more important than ever, it causes people to reappraise everything around them, high art included.

The End of Money Victorianism

Even the most casual observer of contemporary life cannot help but notice how references to money dominate just about every conversation; yet only a few years have gone by since Norman Podhoretz could in all seriousness describe money as "the dirty little secret of American life, surrounded by the same kind of taboos and no-no's as sex in Victorian society." Indeed, this sounds like a fitting description of the way money was considered not too long ago, even as late as the mid-1960s. Most people between thirty and forty years of age can remember their elders discussing money matters in hushed tones, and probably have vivid recollections of stern parental admonitions not to expose the family's money situation (good or bad) to their classmates. Today, things have changed drastically; the Victorian period of money has finally come to an end, and the discussion of money is no more a taboo than that other Victorian no-no, the discussion of sex, even though, as we will see later on, there is still a fair bit of guilt attached to money. It matters little that George Gilder and others still consider that "there are few rules of etiquette so firm as the ban on boasting about salary and income or on confessing the financial spurs and influences in our behavior."[11] This may be true of the circles in which Mr. Gilder revolves, but the more common reality is that the vast majority of people, from the executive suite to the breadline, do not abide by this "rule of etiquette." In the real world, real people, unless they are talking from the pulpit or running for public office, are constantly either boasting or complaining about the amount of money they earn and spend; they readily and proudly proclaim their passion for money.

Over the years, money Victorianism has affected not only individuals but the world of business. Most corporations' public relations still reek of money Victorianism; they stress the company's contributions to the common good, the development of new goods and services, smart engineering, customer satisfaction, technological innovation, contributions to the national security, and the like. Only in their financial reports to their shareholders, which remain relatively "inside" documents, do they boast of their ability to make money. But one look at the internal organization of most corporations indicates the extent to which they have taken a major step beyond the vision of money as a "dirty little secret," as witnessed by the emergence of the finance department as the real seat of power in the typical business operation, after years of dominance by the engineering, sales, and legal departments.

The abandonment in recent years of money Victorianism by individuals and corporations alike points to a fundamental change in money. From a simple adjunct to business, money has become more important than business itself. And for individuals, money has become so exciting that they cannot stop talking about it. It simply does not do to treat it like a secret.

The End of Money Moralism

Perhaps the deepest and most significant change in money attitudes is that money is no longer synonymous with morals and coterminous with the work ethic. In the nineteenth century, even in America, money was mainly considered a measure of one's morality, sociability, and conformity. Robert Reich offers a description of the mentality of that period: "Success was more the product of the proper attitudes than any power or skill."[12] George Gilder perpetuates the moralistic dimensions of money: the individual "values his money because his expenditure of funds is psychologically rooted in his previous expenditure of effort."[13] Clearly, this no longer reflects contemporary reality and attitudes. Every day we meet people who do not feel there is any link whatsoever between their money and their efforts and attitudes, their "hard work and determination," and who do not feel in the least guilty about it. As one successful stockbroker told us, "The only real secret about money is how easy it is to make a lot of it." The traditional money moralism, the consummate expression of which was the Protestant work ethic, is being phased out as money stands more and more on its own, as it is more and more valued for itself and not in conjunction with any "expenditure of effort," nor as a reward for good behavior. There may not be many deserving poor, but there are no deserving rich, either.

Such changes as the end of the money liturgy or of money moralism are not, as is sometimes alleged, the result of mass money hysteria or of collective greed. In fact, they correspond to well-documented, albeit widely misunderstood, changes in "real" money. That the specialists have in general failed to grasp the significance of these changes is another consequence of the separation of the two worlds of money described in the previous chapter: the specialists' notion of money is limited by age-old archetypes and assumptions which are never questioned and which often turn out to be less perceptive, if more statistically detailed and technically involved, than the layperson's intuitions.

The Earth Is Not Flat

The idea that money never changes is a kind of historical flat-landism. Aristotelian geography and cosmology seem quite farcical today, but people who would not be caught dead endorsing Aristotle's physics don't give a second thought about echoing the Aristotelian view that money is "the dead pledge of society"; as Henry Bretton put it, this view of money as "a neutral thing without qualities or life of its own survived by a few hundred years the discovery that the earth was round."[14]

The modern perspective on money is as radically different from the previous notions and attitudes about money as Galileo's cosmology was from Aristotle's. In the world of modern money, money itself, not Fort Knox or your local bank, is at the center of the universe. This is as momentous a change of perspective as the conclusion that the Earth was not the center of the universe.

No matter what monetarists of the strict obedience may say, money's behavior cannot be reduced to simplistic explanations based on the supply/demand model. Money's unique character means that it cannot be considered an ordinary item of international trade or just another tool of foreign policy. Currency speculation is much riskier and has greater impact on the world economy than any kind of commodity trading precisely because money is not just any old commodity; even describing money as a "supercommodity" or as the most desirable commodity of all is to miss the point.

The mythology holds that money is timeless; in the real world, money is timely; the real world is the world of money, where time is money and money is time. Money constantly contradicts received ideas about wealth; this is why money is so often described as being the "source" of so much trouble, especially by the rich. These changes in money also imply changes in the nature of money literacy. What might have been considered money literate behavior one hundred years ago—profitably running an assembly line at breakneck speed while paying low wages—is today's money illiteracy. Money is constantly changing because, at any given moment, money is the expression of the state of development of human interaction.

—————Money Myth 3:—————

Money and Government Are in Cahoots

THE MYTH: Political cunning is the same thing as good money sense. Money and politics are two alternate roads to the summit of social power. Today, as always, a common network of relations and similar methods lead to success in money or politics.

The Myth in Action

Equating politics and money invariably gives money a bad name. Few things turn people off from money more than the assumption that, since politics is a hotbed of corruption and squandering of public funds, making money involves the same set of skewed ethics and questionable operating principles.

America has enjoyed a miserable image abroad ever since the 1960s because the massive misuse of American money by such politicians as the shah of Iran and Ferdinand Marcos was assumed to be representative of the national character of the United States. Vietnam was an even more distressing instance of the same process: people there learned to hate money because they were forced to choose between Ho Chi Minh's totalitarianism and nineteenth-century cesspool capitalism as practiced by the military and the politicians in the South.

Anyone with a normal belief in an honest buck may be quite disgusted with the politicians' disgraceful money practices, but they still feel that they owe something to politicians, and even that they have a certain kinship with them. Rather than questioning the ground rules of the politicians' rationale, they simply look around for the politician closest to their positions on social issues and support this person, even though they share very little except a common money illiteracy.

The confusion between politics and moneymaking has made it possible for countless politicians, social commentators, business leaders, and editorial writers to get very good mileage out of the debate over whether to get government in or out of the way of business. The unanimous proclaimed agenda of business is to minimize government interference in its operations, but business people do not hesitate to attempt to do this by backing all manner of politicians. Meanwhile, the proponents of government, left and right alike, strive to make business more responsive to whatever special interests they represent: the imperatives of national security for conservatives, the needs of the community, the environment, and the poor for liberals. Government ideologues everywhere argue that their particular version of the state is better for business than other political systems and ideologies. Western politicians, conservatives included, insist that their side achieves better socialist results, in the guise of greater wealth for greater numbers of people, than the socialists in Russia and elsewhere; meanwhile, the directors of Gosplan, the Russian central planning bureau, claim they are better at capital formation than the Western capitalists.

Today, hardly anybody is deceived by the continuing show of conservative politicians promising to get government out of the way of business, or by the complementary promises of social reformers to get better government control of business. It is quite obvious, for example, that there will never be less government involvement in a wide range of businesses, if only because of the massive military programs. While different people may take a "business stance" or a "government stance" in debates over deregulation and privatization, there is a strong suspicion that government bureaucrats, prominent journalists, politicians, business leaders, and their lobbyists and PR people all get together in the same bars and restaurants and have a whale of a time. This suspicion of collusion is reinforced by the ease and speed with which some specialists of the revolving door, the Robert McNamaras, the John Connallys, and the Donald Regans move between government and business circles. To conclude from this overwhelming body of evidence that business and government are, if not one and the same thing, at least seriously in cahoots is only normal. And while we would be hard put to disagree with this position, we find ourselves in total disagreement with the sweeping inference often drawn from this conclusion, namely that money and politics are one and the same thing. Few things turn people off from money more than the equation of money with the corruption, influence peddling, and inefficiency that characterize the political process. In addition, the blanket amalgamation of money with politics deprives the individual of any possibility of understanding the government-business nexus. Worse, it taints our grasp of history.

The history of America is routinely offered as the best proof that political savvy and money common sense go hand in hand. America is generally presented as the prime and shining example of a successful association between money and politics as embodied respectively in business and government. The popular notion is that in the beginning the government was an entity somewhat remote from daily life, that the early American government did not get involved in business matters, any more than it did in matters of religion. This beneficial government nonintervention is supposed to have continued, despite some temporary measures made necessary by the Civil War and World War I, until the New Dealers created Big Government as we know it, with its powerful agencies and all-encompassing regulation of business life. Everybody agrees that, if nothing else, Big Government was just what was needed to win World War II. Nowadays, everyone is against Big Government, not out of any deep conviction, but simply because it is too expensive. But it is hard to make any sense of the current debates: the Republicans get elected on an anti–Big Government platform but run a more expensive government than ever, while it is hard to believe that the Democrats would run a more efficient government (and it is at least equally hard to believe that they mean to use government to control the excesses of business). The only way to make sense of the current mess and to cut through the rhetorical fog is to see the relationship between government and business as a continuing one. The history of the business-government relationship is the history of the balancing act of American society between two opposite poles: money and politics.

The Myth Unraveled: American Business and Government Through History, from Philadelphia and Monticello to Wall Street and the Washington Beltway

From the early days of the Republic, the American government was involved in trade and commerce and never restricted itself to the protection of personal freedom; in America the freedom to get products to market was deemed integral to life, liberty, and the pursuit of happiness. The task of developing the continent proved to be a formidable one, beyond the means and resources of any single firm or even of any business consortium (there were no Bechtels at the time). The government provided the coordination without which the building of roads, bridges, and canals would have been intolerably delayed and/or would have become privately owned obstacles to trade, with every road or toll bridge operator charging "whatever the market could bear." The government assisted in every part of the development of the early communications network; it helped secure the foreign loans needed to finance the projects, it took care of the lands acquisitions, and it often supplied the manpower through the Army Corps of Engineers.

The first mass production of rifles, which was to become something of a model for mass production in general, was aided by government funds. "The government's great power to invest and to wait for a return on its investment enabled Eli Whitney [of cotton gin fame] to build his factory and tool up for mass production. This first great triumph of the American businessman was a government-sponsored and government-aided (but not government run) venture."[1]

By the time a transcontinental railroad was needed, a number of companies were physically capable of undertaking the massive effort but still required financial aid from Washington. The statesman/businessman such as Franklin and Hamilton who elegantly wore two hats had become a thing of the past, and companies were controlled by professional businessmen such as the railroad kings—Leland Stanford, Johns Hopkins, and Charles Crocker, who easily got the best of inexperienced government officials. The transcontinental railroad was the first in a series of lucrative government contracts which assured vast fortunes for the railroad builders. "The Union Pacific building westward from the Missouri River was granted 12,000,000 acres of unknown land in alternate sections ten miles deep, and also $27,000,000 in 6%, thirty year government bonds as a first mortage."[2] By 1873 it was clear that outrageous profits were being made and a congressional investigation was initiated.

> In scenes of soaring passion witnessed by galleries packed with the throng of Washington society, bitter recriminations flew back and forth. . . . By fraudulent procedure the first mortgage securing the government's loan of $27,000,000 had been set aside, and a new

first mortgage executed and sold, the proceeds of which
were diverted to the holding company. . . . The tale
of appalling waste, of crime and turpitude shook the
whole country like a mighty quake and set many a
weak structure to rocking. In the bourses panic
seethed; thousands lost their savings in Union Pacific's fall, while distress quickly spread to the grain-
growing regions.[3]

The Interstate Commerce Commission grew out of these
and other hearings which revealed that the government
simply had no way to control the conduct of people it
had given large amounts of money to. The ICC was established as an attempt to make grant recipients financially
responsible in their dealings with the public. In the beginning the role of this first permanent regulatory agency
was largely symbolic. For the first thirty years of its
existence the ICC lacked the means to enforce its decisions, but it still served a purpose for government. The
mere condemnation of the most blatant abuses of business at least made the government seem sensible about
money in comparison. And even though the ICC did little
if anything to halt abuses, the very fact that the agency
was created offered business the opportunity to complain
about government interference in its operations.

By the turn of the century America had professional
business people of world caliber. The Great War saw
the emergence of the first American world-class professional bureaucrats and economic planners. Herbert Hoover,
the U.S. food administrator, also headed the Interallied
Food Council, a commission whose "task was to increase
the production and decrease the consumption of food in
America so that armies and civilians overseas might be
adequately fed. He was empowered to fix the prices of
staples, license food distributors, co-ordinate purchases,
supervise exports, prohibit hoarding or profiteering, and
stimulate production."[4] Other agencies, from the War
Industries Board to the War Finance Corporation and the
War Labor Board, regulated fuel consumption, closed
down industries deemed not essential to the war effort,

settled labor disputes, and saw to the financing of the war. The centralization of economic planning also provided the first comprehensive quantitative picture of business activity as the first national economic statistics were compiled.

For the first time the government became a huge customer for goods and services. "Congress created an emergency fleet corporation with unlimited power and generous funds to requisition, purchase, construct, and operate ships without limitation."[5] Every segment of the business world seemed to benefit. Heads of businesses could concentrate on production while government took care of the headaches of planning, pricing, and generally regulating the economy at large. The American soldiers were better treated and equipped than other armies in the trenches; as for workers who remained at home, their wages rose by some 25 percent during the war.

For all this, the government did not come out of the war as "big government" as we know it; by 1923 "there were only about 70,000 federal employees in Washington" compared with some 2 million federal employees today.[6] After the ad hoc war agencies were disbanded, the main economic tool of the government was the Federal Reserve System, which had yet to evolve into today's powerful entity known as the Fed. But even though the powerful wartime agencies had been dismantled, a core of civil servants had had a taste of real power; they were also respected, since they were widely credited with having engineered a victorious war effort. The Depression provided them with an opportunity to get back in the driver's seat. The Depression was a disaster for the country as a whole but a windfall for government. A number of programs that had been eliminated at the end of World War I, wartime crisis control procedures which had nothing to do with social reform, were reinstated. "Indeed it has been persuasively argued that the models for many programs and practices of the New Deal are to be found in wartime Washington rather than in the proposals of progressive reformers."[7]

The Turning Point: The Great Depression

Most commentators point to economic illiteracy as a major cause of the Great Depression. John Kenneth Galbraith cites "the poor state of economic intelligence. . . . It seems certain that the economists and those who offered economic counsel in the late twenties and early thirties were almost uniquely perverse."[8] Another historian says that the "failure of economic policy is relatively easy [to understand]. . . . we shall cite instance after instance of what, with hindsight, appears as economic illiteracy."[9] Robert McElvaine reflects that "Eric Hobsbawm's characterization of the economic illiteracy of British leaders during the Depression, while perhaps a bit harsh, can be applied as well to their American counterparts. 'Never did a ship founder with a captain and a crew more ignorant of the reasons for its misfortune or more impotent to do anything about it.' "[10] In all these books the consequences of the policies suggested by misinformed economists are presented in great detail. But though the term "economic illiteracy" is bandied about freely as the cause for these mistaken policies, its root cause is never examined. In our opinion what caused the Depression was not a simple case of economic illiteracy on the part of political leaders and money experts— prescribing and using the wrong recipe at the wrong time. The depression was the first major catastrophe caused by mass money illiteracy. The Florida land speculators, the investors large and small who bought stocks on the margin or jumped on the investment trusts bandwagon, major industrialists and bankers who endorsed the overly optimistic prophecies of economists and stockbrokers, all believed in and acted on the same false notions about money. The Great Depression was the day of reckoning for the common money wisdom of the time; no longer could money be easily made on the cavalier assumption that money makes people stupid, that profits are a measure of money sense, and that money is a scarce substance. It is interesting to see how these notions were exposed and the conclusions which were drawn from their abandonment.

Depression Delusion Number One: "Money Makes People Stupid"

Nearly everyone in power in business and in Washington believed that the ever-escalating growth of consumption was the best sign of economic health and that this growth would continue in part because the American people would purchase whatever was put in front of them. Investment strategies and production estimates were based on the notion that consumers lacked the intelligence and the will to resist the pressure sales tactics of real estate and stock market promoters. The same people who as employees were asked to contribute actively to improvements in production were assumed to be basically unintelligent when the time came to spend their money.

The archetypal pre-Depression business deal was the buying and selling of Florida real estate, much of it worthless swampland. The essential ingredient for the kind of operations known as Ponzi schemes was an infinitely large pool of consumers to keep buying and selling a stupid product.

> Palpably, much of the unloved terrain that thus changed hands was as repugnant to the people who bought it as to the passer-by. The buyers did not expect to live on it; it was not easy to suppose that anyone would. But these were academic considerations. The reality was that this dubious asset was gaining in value by the day and could be sold at a handsome profit in a fortnight ... as long as the supply of people who buy with the expectation of selling at a profit continues to be augmented at a sufficiently paid rate to keep prices rising.[11]

Other supposedly more reputable investment schemes run by major brokerage houses and banks were based on a related principle: someone would always invest in a deal if it was initially organized by seemingly money-wise people. Even before the Depression began, these

schemes were running out of new customers and unable
to make payments on the huge loans they secured. The
lesson which business could have learned—when it comes
to money, people learn quickly from the mistakes of others, or, money discourages rather than creates stupidity—
took awhile to sink in.

These schemers were naive enough or stupid enough to
think that they could emulate the success of the speculators of the mid- and late eighteenth century who made
fortunes in the age of iron when information moved slowly
and was the sole property of a few insiders. By the 1920s
the ticker tape, telephone, automobile, and radio made it
possible for many more people to have access to investment information, severely curtailing the privileged position of the insider and making financial setbacks and
gains public with little delay. These speculators, then,
were victims of the notion that money does not change;
money was changing all around them, accelerating its
pace and forcing people to become smarter, thereby de-
priving speculators of their traditional customer base.

Depression Delusion Number Two: "Profits Are a Measure of Money Sense"

American banks invested in Europe according to the
philosophy that short-run profits are always desirable
because they look good on the balance sheet and on the
stockholders' report. "Chase and Guaranty Trust Company, for example, each had placed nearly half of their
capital in German securities. This was, of course, foolish
. . . but the Germans were offering especially high interest
rates and there was a shortage of investment opportunities in the United States."[12] When the German banking
crisis broke out, the consequences were disastrous for all
concerned. Because the banks' goal was defined in terms
of the narrow notion of profits, they failed to look at the
financial soundness of the Germans' propositions, let alone
question the wisdom of investing so heavily in such a
volatile environment as pre-Hitlerian Germany.

Depression Delusion Number Three: "Money Is a Scarce Substance"

All the redistribution strategies of the Depression era, and there were dozens, were based on the notion that the size of the money pie was limited and that the only way to increase the income of the poor was to take money from the rich. "Nearly sixty percent of the poor questioned in a 1935 *Fortune* survey said that the government should not 'allow a man who has investments worth over a million dollars to keep them.' "[13] Fantasies of this kind must have occupied a good deal of the time of the unemployed and the poorly paid, and were certainly the key to the popularity of the redistribution schemes which dominated the programs of populists like Fiorello La Guardia, Robert La Follette, Huey Long, and Upton Sinclair in America, and Mussolini and Léon Blum in Europe.

Business Shakes Hands with the Devil

Instead of coming to terms with its questionable money practices, business let its mistakes be explained by politicians, and chiefly by the greatest professional politician of his time, Franklin Roosevelt. David Halberstam points out that Roosevelt was the first great media manipulator, but more central to his power was his ability to redefine the relationship between government and business.[14]

Whereas Hoover had tended to treat most issues as a question of principles and doggedly to stay the course set by the principles, Roosevelt let the issues and their possible political fallout direct him. A typical example was his farm legislation. Roosevelt was on the side of a group like the farmers so long as they gave him their unconditional support. "Roosevelt required the leaders of all the major farm interest groups to accept the agricultural plan before it was brought to him. This meant that the President could take credit for success, but could shift the blame for the failure to others. Such a plan might not make sense economically, but it was superb politics."[15]

Roosevelt developed a new presidential *modus operandi* which permitted him to say anything no matter how contradictory as long as he presented the promise of progress. His overwhelming power was made possible by the social vacuum created by the temporary eclipse of business; whether he wanted it or not, Roosevelt was entrusted with the protection of the business-government relationship in the face of great popular pressure for drastic change. The President took up the challenge with great gusto, sparing no effort in order to be all things to all people. He unilaterally redefined the relationship between government and business, but in such a way that business was only too happy to go along (not that it had much choice). Business let him accuse them of certain excesses—greed, selfishness, the centralization of power in large, unresponsive corporations—and thereby agreed to be cast as scapegoats in exchange for being left basically alone behind the smoke screen of the New Deal's rhetoric and agitation. A typical Roosevelt speech from 1936, his annual message to Congress, "called upon Congress to 'wage unceasing warfare' against our 'resplendent economic aristocracy' which sought 'power for themselves, enslavement for the public.' . . . He called upon Americans to keep up the fight against 'the forces of privilege and greed.' "[16]

Still, few were fooled by the rhetoric. " 'The President drove the money changers out of the Capitol on March 4th,' a North Dakota congressman complained, 'and they were all back on the 9th.' Even this charge overstated Roosevelt's 'war' on bankers. On the very morning of his inauguration he agreed to consult with leading 'money changers' on how to solve the banking crisis."[17] Business and government were now ready to embark on their most momentous joint venture.

The Bottom Line: The Real New Deal Was the Manhattan Project

Fighting World War II was the biggest collective project yet undertaken by America. Since the agencies set up to promote the recovery could be readily adapted to the organization of the war effort, it seemed natural for the government to take the lead by once again becoming the main customer for the economy, and by extending its powers of regulation and planning to every sector of activity. The result was the creation of what Seymour Melman has called a permanent war economy.

Not only did government manage the economy in detail, it also provided a strong organizational model for business as a whole. The massive and highly secretive Manhattan Project, which created the A-bomb, pioneered many of the techniques which were to be the cornerstones of business management after the war: multilayered chains of command, systems analysis, intense specialization, compartmentalization on a need-to-know basis, wholesale waste and inefficiency excused by the achievement of a single spectacular result. The graduates of these and other large-scale government undertakings entered business and quickly rose to positions of power based partly on their wide experience in crisis management and their ability to perform under pressure.

The use of management techniques derived from the military even spread to businesses not directly dependent on government work. What was basically a technical exercise in military logistics, scarcity management, and national mobilization was simply transplanted into civilian life under the guise of business administration, most notably by the post-1945 managers who had been to business school on the G.I. Bill. The postwar civilian power structure looked strangely like the wartime chain of command. Eisenhower, the former commander in chief, soon became president and general manager of the country, the ex-officers occupied management positions in various corporate hierarchies more or less according to the old chain of command, and the ex-enlisted men were workers.

At this stage, business not only was a senior partner in the U.S. power structure but was actually operating according to the same techniques used by the other members of the power structure, the government and the military. The problem with using the same management techniques as the government and the army is that it tends to alienate the kind of independent, innovative, critical minds indispensable to the development of new ideas and technologies. However, businesses which yield to pressures to innovate are liable to lose their standing as part of the power structure.

During the Vietnam War, business found itself in this kind of "damned if you do, damned if you don't" predicament. It could either go along with the politicians' line and insult the intelligence of the rising generation, or it could dissent and miss out on the immediate war profits. Business massively adhered to the gospel according to the White House and the Pentagon, and eventually suffered the consequences: a large number of young people turned their backs on a corporate world which they not only identified with the nonsense of the military-industrial complex but also came to see as drab, uninteresting, and generally opposed to any kind of change, including potentially lucrative new projects.

Only after the trauma of Vietnam had receded did the baby boom generation begin to have any kind of influence on the organization of business, often introducing in the corporation techniques pioneered by the protest movement for the facilitation of more direct and open communication, such as rotating leadership and a minimum of hierarchical formality. After years of spinning their wheels in endless meetings to create agendas for government projects that were never funded, or to organize rallies that somehow never attracted enough media attention to be effective, or to figure out why not everyone wanted to take out the commune's garbage, this generation was actually getting things done.

Some businesses, sensing that the way to profits in the post-Vietnam environment was to mend their bridges with youth, had finally started to listen to what the new generation had to say. At last there were signs of the end of the dominance of the honorably discharged platoon commanders over the moneymaking process, with the rediscovery that there could be a more profitable and rewarding way of doing business than the traditional corporate-governmental method. Traditional businesses were being challenged by new kinds of ventures which were becoming huge successes with total disregard for the kind of governmentalized business ethic of yesteryear. Their lasting success in fields ranging from computers to food processing indicates that the kind of Manhattan Project organization which has for so long been business gospel is no longer the best way to do things, especially when you are functioning without reference to the world of government contracts. This was a revelation to traditional business, and came as such a shock that it precipitated the current rampant identity crisis of American business.

The most common cure offered for the business identity crisis is to repeat ad nauseam the traits which characterize healthy and unhealthy businesses. This is somewhat like a therapist telling a patient having a nervous breakdown that a healthy person acts a certain way which is not the way he or she is now acting. The current strengths and shortcomings of American corporate management have been cataloged by Peter Drucker as well as by a new wave of management analysts. Their "critique" of American business reminds us that dedication to research, a quality product, a happy labor force, and satisfied customers usually lead to profits. Of course, this approach is not original; it was the basic credo of Edison and Ford.

The first reflex of anyone suffering from an identity crisis is to look around for an apparently healthy role model. But this knee-jerk reaction only obscures the real problems which led to this identity crisis. American business, in its quest for a role model, turned first to Japan, then to the entrepreneurial sectors of the domestic economy. The management gurus felt vindicated: their ideas, which had been exiled to Japan or adopted by some of the more innovative ventures, were coming back to bail out the ailing industrial giant.

But the identity crisis of American business is not caused by the inability of American companies to make quality products, to create corporate cultures, to get back to basics, or to identify their market niches. These are but symptoms of a much deeper malaise: we are in the middle of the disintegration of the business-government nexus. Practitioners of business are groping in the dark for a way to distance themselves from the government's way of doing things. Management theories come and go; yesterday's acclaimed breakthrough quickly becomes today's faddish failure largely because the business therapists address everything but the essential differences between the universe of money and that of politics. The world of politics is a world of procrastination, of forced consensus, of planned obsolescence, and of secrecy, while money is characterized by decisiveness, diversity, and multiple choices, progress through error, the willingness to give anyone and anything a second chance, and a commitment to openness; above all, the universe of money is a universe of average people acting with a concern for the long term, while the sphere of politics is that of great men obsessed with the short term.

Procrastination and Decisiveness

Politics is the realm of symbolic and highly codified behavior, of rigidly enforced protocol, of good intentions, of innuendos and diplomatic communiqués subject to endless interpretations and misinterpretations ("Finally, the Russians are talking about talking" and "We think we really sent them a message today"), of moral posturing (for example, the debates in Congress over military aid to various rebels in various foreign countries), and of barely disguised rehashes of previously rejected concepts, proposals, and schemes. This institutionalized chaos and confusion, while horrible for us citizens, is actually beneficial to politicians, since it makes the job of evaluating the performance of a particular administration or a particular politician extremely difficult. As Richard Darman, assistant secretary of the treasury and an acknowledged master politician put it, "The trick is to arrange a context in which several competing politicians can step forward together to simultaneously share what credit and blame there is for something that's going to be at least ambiguous."[18] Money-makers, whatever their momentary lapses into indecision, move toward the clarification of ambiguity and confusion because their activity is constantly measured by an unambiguous criterion: If it makes money, it survives; if it doesn't, it disappears. The seeming vulgarity and simplicity of this criterion is actually one of money's greatest strengths.

Consensus and Multiplicity

Reaching a consensus and enforcing adherence to it is the goal of politicians. In all legislatures, questions of all kinds are debated until finally a course of action is chosen which manages to satisfy a number of special interests. Once consensus is achieved, it becomes the sole course of action permitted. American advocates of a strong defense cite the lack of agreement on an aggressive arms policy as a source of weakness. They would much prefer the solid consensus on defense policy which exists in the USSR.[19] Once again, as with Vietnam, the choice is to buy the whole strategy or eventually chance being called a security risk.

Attempts to impose the narrow choices typical of the political arena on consumers always fail. "Buy Black" or "Buy American" are impossible requests for today's smart shoppers; that old Wall Street adage "Buy what you invest in" means nothing to today's shareholders. Investors who hold a portfolio of, say, IBM, General Motors, and People Express stock will not hesitate for a second before they buy an Apple computer, a BMW, or fly first-class on a full-service airline if they feel like it.

Politics is a closed system which leaves no place for diversity, where the choices are severely limited. Not only are the political parties so similar as to offer little or no choice, whatever competition there is between governmental entities nearly always leads to disaster. For instance, in the armed forces, the most common result of the interservice rivalry is that the army, navy, and air force develop identical weapons systems and insist on deploying them simultaneously and without coordination. The same kind of overlapping jurisdiction, parallel structures, and lack of coordination prevails among the competing regulators of banking and finance; the imbroglio between the SEC, the FDIC, the Fed, and the FSLIC over whose turf is whose has already contributed to general confusion and near catastrophes, with no end in sight.

Infallibility and Progress Through Error

Politicians keep repeating the same errors because they view admitting any mistake as a sign of fundamental weakness. Ronald Reagan has yet to admit an error since he started running for office (he's been misquoted and misinterpreted, but never caught messing up), while Walter Mondale has stated publicly that, if given a second chance, he would have changed almost nothing about his disastrous 1984 campaign. The current literature on Vietnam demonstrates the tightrope which the politicians must walk in order to write the history of a blatant failure without admitting to serious errors. Some even proudly proclaim that the United States won the war. General Westmoreland spent six months in court in 1985 trying to prove that he had not erred in estimating enemy troop strength, hoping to pass the buck and to save face. Saving face or passing the buck does not work in the realm of money because the longer errors go undetected and uncorrected the costlier they become. Money is concerned with results, not reputations.

Planned Obsolescence and Recycling

Politics is the realm of brutal, instant, and irreversible obsolescence. Politicians are always fascinated by the promise of a breakthrough or drastic change. That is why they are so fond of weaponry such as that of the Strategic Defense Initiative which renders utterly useless the massive investments of yesteryear. Money, on the other hand, gives people and ideas a second chance. Regularly the styles of entire decades are brought back into fashion, giving a new commercial life to clothing, furniture, music, hairstyles, and automobiles from that period. Money even gives weapons a second chance. Old rifles, tanks, and jeeps keep getting recycled, most of the time harmlessly, on the international weapons market long after they have been disowned by the military, while the army doesn't even bother to turn spent shell casings into ashtrays.

Secrecy and Openness

Secrecy is no longer an essential ingredient of business practice, especially in the high-technology sectors. While an understandable degree of discretion still surrounds the actual research and development work on new products in the computer and electronics industry, it makes good business sense to put as much of the operating systems, systems architecture, and the like in the public domain as soon as, and often before, the product comes to market. For the government, on the other hand, secrecy is not an aberration or a necessary evil; it is essential.

In government circles, security clearances are not only a way of life but the surest indication of one's position in the hierarchy: your power is measured by the number and quality of secrets to which you have access. The ability and determination to keep secrets is increasingly the hallmark of the modern politicians and civil servants.

William Clark's greatest achievement as secretary of the interior was keeping his department out of the limelight; according to many observers, his main quality was "obscurity."[20] Most commentators agree that John Poindexter got the job of national security adviser in November of 1985 basically because he knows how to keep his mouth shut: "When asked whether he would be as accessible to reporters as his predecessor was, he smiled and said 'maybe.' "[21] And the Watergate affair gave ample proof that, if anything, the political parties are more paranoid and obsessed with secrecy than the government itself.

The rise of former intelligence chiefs to high political office is indicative of the vital importance of the management of secrets for modern-day governments. For example, George Bush, the American Vice-President (and presidential hopeful), is a former head of the CIA. The late Yuri Andropov, before he became the number one man in the Kremlin, was chief of the KGB. Only in politics do secrecy specialists rise to the top: in most businesses, directors of security are not generally prime candidates for the position of chief executive officer.

Moreover, the motives for the imposition of more and more secrecy stem from the internal logic of the government, and this logic is beyond the understanding of civilians. Typical of the growing catch-22 rationale for secrecy are the explanations of a CIA official who, when asked the reasons for the secrecy classification of a certain communications satellite, said, "You know, I can't give you any reason behind it, except that it's part and parcel of the whole satellite question. The decision has been made to maintain the classification and that's all we can say."[22] In other words, the reasons for secrecy are secret.

In the past, business generally went along with increased secrecy measures, but recent attempts to expand the realm of classified material have been met by increasing resistance from business. A well-known instance is the Pentagon's attempt to restrict the export of more and more high-technology products to the East and to Europe even though its possible military applications are often difficult to demonstrate. There is a growing realization that this kind of secrecy is counterproductive beyond just the loss of sales which result from embargoes: fundamental scientific research, for example, is clearly jeopardized because the Defense Department is trying to limit scientific exchange in nonclassified fields, even with traditional partners like Britain and West Germany.[23] Of more immediate concern to businesses that are even remotely involved in government work is that employees with one kind of security clearance can't converse freely with those who have a different clearance, and the climate of paranoia which develops is detrimental to a creative atmosphere. Information which should circulate freely cannot because the government has defined it as too sensitive. Massive amounts of time and money are devoted to creating a parallel, hierarchic organization designed to dovetail with the government and military hierarchies and to meet their secrecy standards. The benefits of all this activity are at best dubious and often detrimental:

> A young engineer was employed by an aerospace firm and assigned the task of preparing cost and price estimates for new products on which the firm would submit bids to the Department of Defense. In doing this work he was expressly prohibited from having any access to or communication with the accounting department. Neither was he permitted to read any of the firm's own internal accounting reports. Hence, he had no information available on the details of previous costs of similar work. . . . This sort of job requirement proved to be unnerving to the engineer in question, because his training instilled in him values about efficiency which he was unable to fulfill under the conditions imposed upon him. After a few years, he left this job in disgust.[24]

Great Men and Average Men

Political history is the history of magnanimous and far-seeing presidents and statesmen, of brilliant generals, of impassioned revolutionaries, of great individuals destined to do great things. The common person is relegated to a minor role as part of an obedient constituency, as a faceless member of an unruly mob, or as a casualty in a tragic war. But the history of money reads more like the history of the common person. By and large money is made, spent, invested, managed, misused, and made productive by average people holding average jobs and running average companies. A composite profile of the average successful money-maker has been compiled by Thomas Stanley of Georgia State University who, according to *The Wall Street Journal,* has surveyed thousands of millionaires. "The high-profile leisure class shows up as a minority in Mr. Stanley's research. Much more common is the owner of the small business—a string of dry cleaning stores, hamburger franchises or travel agencies."[25] This average world of money is often invisible to politicians and to many in business, who despite their pollsters measuring consumer behavior and political preference, generally insist that trends can only be created by imitating trendsetters (the great men and women at the top) and who are not able to spot a trend until they can identify a trendsetter who could have created this new behavior.

Money and politics operate according to two utterly different and irreconcilable time frames. The politician lives from election to election and from one opinion poll to the next. The politicians' long term is the two- or four-year period until the next election, and the short term is tomorrow's press conference. Money, on the other hand, is made over time. Long-range strategy and patience are of the essence.

The Current State of Business and of Government

Given the growing perception of a hiatus in the traditional business-government alliance, the government prefers to simply put itself beyond criticism by preempting it. When government institutions are attacked for their inefficiency, government answers with slogans like "get government out of people's lives" and programs for privatizing a number of government functions.

Although privatization may change a few superficial aspects of former government functions, it doesn't alter the nature of the privatized activity. The bulk of privatization consists of business taking over security matters, including the running of penal institutions and supplementing and eventually replacing the traditional police forces with private police officers and private investigators. This does not guarantee any degree of change. For example, consider what happens when the running of prisons is contracted out to security firms: not only are the cost savings for taxpayers dubious, there is no basic improvement in the daily life of the prisoner. Prison remains a crucible of money illiteracy, and ex-prisoners return to the streets with as little knowledge about how to survive—that is, how to deal with money—as they went in. Rather than being an avenue of social progress and of the reduction of government presence, privatization results in an increasing number of businesses acting like the government, defending institutions and traditions they might have otherwise questioned. The end result is not less government but simply less obvious government.

The End of the New Deal Is No Big Deal

The current political refrain heard from every quarter is that New Deal liberalism has been a failure. The proclaimed political agenda of the two political parties is to correct the mistakes of that era. It is never quite clear, though, exactly what the New Deal accomplished. As we have seen, the various agencies and institutions which conjure up the image of Big Government did not originate in the New Deal years, but during the Great War and under Hoover. The only real innovation of the New Deal was to turn the government into a high-profile operation. This is seen by today's politicians as the biggest mistake of all times. They long for a government which can operate in quiet fashion out of the spotlight, away from annoying auditors, oversight committees, and investigative reporters.

In both business and government circles the identity crisis of American business and the larger issue of the future of America are largely discussed in terms of more or less regulation, more or less foreign trade, more or less protectionism. These are the same kinds of dead ends as privatization. Because they avoid looking at the central problem, whatever debate there is on the future of American business in the next few years is likely to consist of the same kind of drivel.

Toward Money Literacy: Submitting Business and Government to the Money Test

The root cause of the current identity crisis of business is that, after years of suppression by the urgency of largely fabricated foreign crises, the incompatibility of politics and money is affecting everyone's money. Companies see their bottom lines adversely affected by government priorities, and individuals see such personal financial essentials as their old-age pensions seriously jeopardized by politicians who have for years used these issues requiring long-range planning for short-term electoral benefits. These problems are surfacing now because of the new money awareness. Ever since the war in Asia, there has been a distancing of the younger generation from government.

This new generation, which was born into a world of money and which has practiced it with a certain success, came to evaluate the impact of government according to money criteria, especially since the government insisted on presenting itself as the national repository of money wisdom. The government and the traditional businesses patterned after it have been subjected to the test of money and they have failed. The current money-oriented generation is acutely aware of the shortcomings of both; it is just as busy debunking the old business credo by inventing new ways to make money as it is utterly unimpressed by the available political choices. The unprecedented amount of money which this generation has had access to, coupled with its more adult relationship to this money, rather than leading to a renewal of the cushy deal between traditional business and traditional politics, has only heightened the caustic effect of money on politics described by Henry Bretton: "As money moves . . . into what we traditionally call politics, it turns into a corrosive and dissolving agent, disorganizing, destabilizing, even subverting the political system it is presumed to serve."[26] Such are the effects of money literacy. Nostalgics of the old ways may deplore this; we see it as a glimmer of hope, a pillar of sanity in the coming years.

——Money Myth 4:——

Money Causes War

THE MYTH: The surest and quickest cure for an ailing economy is a good war. A nation's money future depends on its determination to maintain a strong military and to use it when deemed appropriate. Money, the sinews of war, fans man's bellicose instincts. Money not only thrives on war but actually pushes otherwise peaceful nations and people toward it. The money men have always been staunch supporters of war; they manipulate governments into devoting huge sums to war preparations and eventually into going to war, enriching themselves at every step of the process, most noticeably by making the weapons which ordinary people use to slaughter each other.

The Myth in Action

The belief that money causes wars leads to lumping all successful money-makers together as staunch, unconditional allies and supporters of the military and of their perpetual war effort (which, these days, goes under the euphemism of "defense"). Since the two groups control all the traditional means of persuasion (weapons and money, bullets and ballots), there is no way to turn them away from the arms race and to force them to work for peace, except by appealing to the humanitarian instincts of the world's politicians and business leaders, the very approach which has proved so ineffective since antiquity. Because there is nothing keeping the bellicose tendencies of the military in check, even the most peaceful, innocuous, least military-related moneymaking activities are viewed as a form of resignation, a second-rate activity, an admission of impotence in the face of the world of geopolitics, which ultimately determines the future of the human race. The pitiful result of this attitude is that the quest for lasting peace has come to be symbolized by the ragtag crowds of peace marchers who are sure to prove as ineffective at stopping the arms race as their predecessors of twenty and fifty years ago were in preventing previous wars. Worse, the idea that money and warmongering go hand in hand also pervades the business ideology. Despite the more level-headed, quintessential money-inspired opinion that "nuclear war can ruin your career," whenever push comes to shove the tendency remains for business as a group to fall in line and rally around the military's agenda whenever the words "national interest" are uttered, especially if there is the perspective of lucrative and exclusive contracts.

The Myth Unraveled: Money as Peacekeeper

Money has never caused wars. On the contrary, it has consistently tended to prevent wars or to limit their scope. In order to go to war, governments have always been forced to beg, borrow, or steal huge sums of money. This is as true of today's rulers as it was of the Roman emperors and the satraps of ancient Greece. The one thing that has limited wars is that they are expensive; in many cases, hostilities which could have gone on for years and years were cut short for money reasons. War is and always has been caused by men of state who managed to sidestep the limits imposed on their martial instinct by the levelheaded logic of money. When a government sets out to drum up enthusiasm for war in its population, it never does so through an open discussion of the costs of going to war, but appeals to the so-called higher values of patriotism, religion, or concern for the national interest. If governments were to present to their populations realistic budget projections before engaging in a military adventure, the taxpayers would vote against war every time.

From Professional Armies to Total War

Up until the nineteenth century, wars were rather limited affairs fought between professional armies on battlefields reserved for that purpose, and the civilian population was largely left alone. For centuries the size of armies remained quite small; it is reported that at the battle of Leuctra in 371 B.C., Epaminondas' army of some 5,000 defeated a force of 10,000 Spartans. More than a millennium later at Hastings, roughly the same numbers of combatants would be involved, with Harold, the king of England, and William the Conqueror each heading a force of about 8,000. Of course, there were some exceptions; for instance, it is said that Darius, the emperor of Persia, met Alexander the Great's army with 200,000 men. There is no doubt that such a vast army could only be assembled because Darius, an archetypal antic despot, did not have to abide by rules of fiscal responsibility.

Up until the eighteeneth century, the conquering appetites and bellicosity of monarchs, generals, and *condottieri* had been constrained by their ability to pay their soldiers, which was determined in turn by the size of their treasury, that is to say, by their skill at increasing taxes without being overthrown; they were chafing at the bit because a ceiling had seemingly been reached in revenue raising. Military commanders, eager to step into the power vacuum created by the Age of Revolution, were looking for a way to fight large-scale wars without regard for expenses. Napoleon Bonaparte, the scion of what would be described today as a Corsican Mafia family, managed to establish himself as emperor of France and squared the circle of affordable large-scale war by inventing the modern way of war, the so-called total war. This new way of waging war involved the total mobilization of a nation's resources and population and ruthless treatment of the enemy, its land, and its citizenry. In this kind of war, a government's only investment was, in principle, the original outfitting of troops which would afterward support themselves; once equipped at their government's expense, the troops were to live off the enemy's land, something which had until then been the exception rather than the rule.

The advent of total war was marked by a quantum leap in the scope of battles, as can be seen by looking at the evolution of the strength of armies between 1700 and 1800. In 1704 at Blenheim, the adversaries, Marlborough and Tallard, fielded some 56,000 soldiers between them, a number consistent, given the increase in population, with the standards set in the days of Epaminondas and William the Conqueror. But within fifty years, a marked increase took place: at Leuthen in 1757 Frederick the Great's 36,000 troops faced some 70,000 Austrians. This was the kind of battle and the size of forces which inspired the young Napoleon. Barely half a century later at Austerlitz, Napoleon's forces alone were almost half again as numerous as the combined total of Blenheim (he had front-line forces of 53,000 and more than 20,000 in reserve), while his opponents had some 90,000 troops, with as many reinforcements waiting in the wings.[1]

Of course, even Napoleon could only defy the logic of money for so long, and eventually he very nearly ruined France with his imperialistic escapades. Even though his plan was to wage war on the cheap, the costs turned out to be enormous, especially since his kind of empire building, unlike that of Spain, Britain, or the Netherlands, was carried out with no consideration whatsoever for industry and commerce. Bonaparte could barely read or write, let alone figure out a balance sheet, and the main objective of his conquests was to keep the chieftains of his mafia happy. To achieve this, he squandered what was left of France's treasury and got the best part of the country's youth killed. He ended up selling what would undoubtedly have become France's greatest asset, Louisiana, in order to finance his last plundering expeditions. The peace, however brief, which followed Waterloo was literally brought about by money: ultimately, it was the Rothschilds' millions, siding with Britain and its allies, which brought the Napoleonic juggernaut of devastation to a stop.

Nevertheless, Bonaparte's concept of people's war, as codified by one of his opponents, the Prussian strategist Carl von Clausewitz, was to become the inspiration for all the subsequent cost-no-object theories of warfare; guerrilla warfare, Blitzkrieg, "people's wars," counterinsurgency operations, and other contemporary woes all have their common origin in the Napoleonic system of war. Beyond specific doctrines of war, the most deleterious legacy of the Napoleonic era was the preposterous notion that being at war was a normal state of affairs; this became accepted logic for the next 130 years of European history. The impression of a permanent state of war was further reinforced because it seemed that the whole world was at war, if not at home, then in the colonies, as country after country tried to grab a piece of Asia, Africa, or the Indian subcontinent.

War in Exile: Colonial Wars in the Nineteenth Century

The money imperative is widely assumed to have been the driving force behind the colonial expeditions of the eighteenth and nineteenth centuries. The common view is that the advanced nations of the period, not only the European powers but also America and Japan, had so much money that they had no place to invest it and, in order to make a profit, had to force foreign, often primitive, nations into their commercial orbit by force of arms. This assumption is the basis for the conventional description of imperialism as a more or less virulently racist system of super-exploitation orchestrated by scheming capitalists and merchants who were free to call in the gunboats should the natives get restless. However convenient, reassuring, and widely accepted this interpretation of the colonial era may be, it does not correspond to reality. The blame for the dreadful period of colonial wars and expeditions should not rest on money, but rather on the lack of money in the advanced nations. This lack of money was the root cause of the empire-building fantasies of soldiers and politicians. Frustrated Bonapartes turned to "virgin territories," usually those closest to wherever they happened to be stationed, as described by the British historian Paul Johnson:

> Japanese military expansion was often dictated by assertive military commanders on the spot, who exceeded or even disobeyed the orders of the ruling group. That was the French pattern too. Algeria was acquired as a result of army insubordination. Indo-China had been entered by overweening naval commanders; it was the marines who got France involved in West Africa. In one sense the French Empire could be looked upon as a gigantic system of outdoor relief for army officers . . . any notion of "finance capital" desperately looking for colonies as places to invest its huge surpluses of capital is preposterous. There was never such a thing as surplus capital. Investment capital was always hard to come by, but especially in the colonies. The tropics did not yield big returns until the very end of the colonial era.[2]

Once the military had launched a colonial operation, individual business people, especially those who were not too successful in the old country, thought up patriotic or moral justifications to get involved, or saw the colonies as an opportunity to make a quick profit. Presented with the *fait accompli* of a colonial system already set up by their military commanders, such entrepreneurs simply took the line of least resistance and set out to try to make the most of a situation over which they had little control, making every effort to turn it into a profitable, if not entirely sound, business proposition. Meanwhile, back in Europe, refined through a series of events which had included the Franco-Prussian War, fighting in Italy and the Balkans as well as the Crimean War, total war was about to rear its ugly head once again, and with more devastating consequences than ever.

World War I

World War I is generally portrayed as the golden age of the war profiteers, a period dominated by the Krupps, the Schneiders, and the Duponts, loathsome figures which make the members of today's "military-industrial complex" seem like peaceniks. It is true that the so-called Great War was much more devastating than anything before (and, nuclear bombings aside, since), but this is not because it was aimed at making money for the cannon kings. What made that war so murderous was that it was an old-fashioned total war, where kings and emperors and tsars were trying to settle their family quarrels by shedding their subjects' blood without any regard for the cost involved. The Great War was the last nineteenth-century war, a war precipitated by the collapse of the Austro-Hungarian and Russian empires, and more generally of the post-Napoleonic European order established by the Vienna treaties.

"In Flanders fields the poppies blow / Between the crosses, row on row / That mark our place / We are the dead. . . ."[3] To this day the grim refrain recalls how thousands and thousands of lives were wasted in savage and senseless hand-to-hand combat over a few hundred square miles of farmland. None of the general staffs, none of the available weaponry, had brought deliverance from the quagmire of trench warfare and the atrocities of gas attacks. The most formidable and the most expensive war machines of all times were proving utterly worthless: the greatest naval engagement in history, the battle of Jutland, was nothing but a costly stalemate. Drew Middleton, noting that at the battle of Verdun, "the total butcher's bill probably was around 800,000 . . . in an area no larger than Burlington, Vermont," describes the general feeling in 1917: "Sunk in the mud and caught on the barbed wire was the theory and practice of war as it had hitherto been fought."[4] With the notable exception of Woodrow Wilson's America, which had only entered the war very late in the game and which had not suffered the devastation of war at home, every European country came out of the war humiliated and/or broke.

"The war to end all wars" was not, because the outcome of the war was seen in terms of national pride, with the result that governments wasted the years from 1918 to 1939 licking the wounds inflicted on their countries' egos. Because of this, while postwar Europe desperately needed a major injection of money, its financial resources were channeled either toward war reparations or toward rearmament. Few fortunes had actually been made during the war; rather, old fortunes were consolidated, and the development of new industries not dependent on the military was stifled. Worse, innovation in post-1918 Europe was nearly impossible because the war had left Europe's infrastructure in a shambles; most notably, the occupation of the Ruhr by foreign troops paralyzed the continent's most advanced heavy industry.

Deprived by an antiquated monetary system built on the gold standard of the funds they needed for reconstruction, desperate nations took shelter in outdated concepts of mercantilism and protectionism. The world had come out of the worst shooting war on record only to find itself bogged down in a series of trade wars which further limited the growth of money. The effects were awesome: between 1929 and 1933, with protectionism rampant, world trade shrank by a factor of 6, from almost $3 billion to around $500 million, and speculation reinforced money paranoia.[5]

The fiscal, monetary, and financial fiascoes of the period were not recognized for what they were, the result of growth-stifling, war-oriented economic policies; instead, they were ascribed to the implacable logic of money. Money baiting became a growth industry. Most countries were plagued by demagogues, and some, most notably Spain, Italy, Germany, China, and Japan, were ruled by whatever political gang happened to prevail; the common denominator of these gangsters was their contempt for money. The most notorious were of course the German Nazis; their anti-Semitism was simply the most repugnant expression of their hatred of money. The Nazis' anti-Semitism was the continuation of a German tradition going back at least as far as Luther; it consisted first and foremost of blind animosity toward Jews because they were traditionally the people most closely associated with money.

American Isolationism: Business and the American Way of War

One of the most blatant instances of money's opposition to war was the traditional opposition of many prominent members of the American business community to their country's military expeditions. This reticence probably had its roots in the reminiscences of the Civil War. Even though many business people had profited from the war, they were all too aware that the thousands of commercial and financial improprieties which had surfaced during the war would never have come into being in times of business as usual, of business not entirely and essentially centered around the government. J. P. Morgan had been strongly opposed to the Spanish-American War; the country had only entered the Great War after much reluctance (and under the excuse of making the world "safe for democracy") and had stayed out of such episodes as the Spanish Civil War entirely; in every instance, prominent business people had been active opponents of American involvement, and now people like Henry Ford were in favor of isolationism in the face of the Nazi threat to Europe. Such an attitude on the part of the business community was the norm rather than the exception. It had nothing to do with insensivity to world affairs or with humanistic pacifism; business leaders opposed to war were expressing the incompatibility between money and war. As James Schlesinger (who should know, having been defense secretary) noted, "It is a matter of historical record that the business community is regularly the first to depart from the defense consensus. Unlike the general public, it recognizes that building defenses costs money."[6]

America refused to be involved in the war in 1939 for the good reason that it made no sense in terms of money; there were no big profits to be made from the war, mostly because American industry was not geared toward arms production. When the hostilities broke out in 1939, they were seen by most Americans as a strictly European affair, which indeed they were: taking care of unfinished business going all the way back to Napoleon, Wellington, and Metternich, a kind of uglier replay of the tragedy of 1914. This was the very nightmare from which immigrants had fled when they sailed toward Ellis Island. Turning their backs on Europe and its seemingly endless series of wars, they had taken up the pursuit of money in the new land as an alternative, and the Old World's quarrels were seen as having little or no relationship with this new life and were therefore ignored.

Europe's war evolved into a world war when hostilities broke out in the Pacific. America did not enter the war with an eye to conquest or to increase its influence in world affairs; because of its superior technology and wealth, America was already the center of the world in nearly every respect. Neither did it join the fray because of its alliances, because it needed "living space," or in a desperate bid to rejuvenate its economy; the outbreak of war did not even play a major role in the post-Depression recovery, which was already under way.

The unique characteristic of the American way of war was its businesslike approach to warfare. Most American commanders, unlike their European and Asian counterparts, were not aristocratic nostalgics operating with a lofty disregard for the national treasury or the lives of their troops. The MacArthurs and the Eisenhowers thought of the G.I.'s as workers, who if they were treated properly and equipped with the proper tools, would get the job done, that is, produce the expected tactical and strategic results; their own job and that of their staff was to supply competent management and draw up sensible and economical plans. By and large, their priority was to bring the boys back alive quickly so they could go back to work.

America had essentially sent troops overseas to stop the war in what was basically a police action designed to put an end to senseless killing and massive destruction of productive resources rather than a patriotic mobilization aimed at protecting the nation's industrial heartland and its vital supply lines. Even in victory, America behaved like no other world power had ever done. American armies and technology had achieved unprecedented military victory over the Axis powers, but the political structure of Europe and of the Far East had been left largely intact; even the occupation of Japan was a benign affair, more like political reform than military government. Yet American intervention had been so massive and overwhelming that the ultimatum delivered, not merely to the Axis powers but to all of Europe and Asia, was clear: behave or else; this time around our armies came and conquered, but left your national identities intact; but should there be one more round of nationalistic, chauvinistic nonsense, there will be some drastic changes made. The American forces delivered money's warning: the world can't afford war.

The Aftermath of World War II

America's participation in the war had not been a simple case of Roosevelt spending America out of the Depression while lining the pockets of defense contractors, but an almost necessary step in a kind of informal worldwide money literacy campaign waged by America: it had seemed

that the only way to create the preconditions for money
growth was to force them down the throats of the rest of
the world, and this had necessitated the creation of a
powerful military machine. The problem with the war-is-
good-for-the-economy argument is that the Second World
War was a one-of-a-kind situation. The American presence in World War II is a unique case in modern history
of weapons of war serving the cause of money literacy.

Unlike the Europeans and the Japanese, Americans had
not had the firsthand experience of the devastation of
their own country in the course of the two world wars.
For them, war did not carry the notion of fighting to
protect one's home and one's own immediate homeland.
For Americans, the ugliness of war was essentially a foreign phenomenon; there had certainly been a number of
American casualties, but the massive devastation had
taken place overseas; on the home front the war years
had basically been a time of more and more business as
usual, like collecting overtime for a sixty-hour workweek.
This, even more than the proper treatment of the G.I.'s
by their commanders, had made the war an acceptable
proposition. Before the war, Americans had been very
leery of any form of military involvement, especially in
other people's wars; World War II had not really changed
that outlook. Except for a few psychopaths and chroni-
cally unemployable, people were very happy to go back
to the normal, civilian life. The speed and scope of the
postwar demobilization was impressive: by 1946 the
11-million-strong wartime army had been drastically reduced to a mere 1.6 million.

Of course, many had come to the conclusion that, since
the war had somehow been profitable, a continuing commitment to large military outlays was a good investment.
More than the general public, the business community
fell victim to the belief that the postwar prosperity was
due to America having undertaken a war and won it,
conquering Europe and the Far East in the traditional,
military sense of the word. It was easy to infer from the
outcome of World War II that America could enter just
about any war and win it, with desirable economic fall-

out both during and after the war. Seymour Melman offers this description of the militaristic postwar hubris:

> At the close of the Second World War the men of the American Establishment saw themselves as chiefs of the preeminent military and economic power in the world. This confidence was based on the visible evidence of massive destruction in other principal industrial areas of the world as contrasted with the intact population base and industrial machine of the United States. It was assumed that with American scientific and technical know-how, a monopoly in nuclear power and the availability of almost unlimited funds, the United States could surely hold position as Number One military power, using that power for worldwide political control.[7]

However, since the criterion generally used to proclaim that the war had been "good" was the level of prosperity achieved, the foundations were laid for the public to evaluate future wars in terms of money. Americans had intuitively begun to judge war in money terms and they would continue to do so despite the overwhelming glut of nationalistic, supposedly anticommunist propaganda churned out by the government since the early 1950s in order to justify what was an entirely new experience for America: systematic and massive preparations for war. The first and crucial battle for strategic nuclear weapons that Curtis LeMay and Dean Acheson had to wage was fought on the money front; they got all the support they needed from Leon Keyserling, then head of the recently created Council of Economic Advisers, who assured all and sundry that as much as 20 percent of the United States gross national product could go to the defense budget without seriously affecting the nation's economy.[8]

During the two decades which began with the Korean War and ended with the fiasco of Vietnam, business was just about totally taken in by the promise of military work as a gravy train and of the use of military force as the best way to secure, if only symbolically, supplies and markets. This led it to endorse military expenditures and wars which ultimately undermined America's position as leader of the world's business community. This was truly a case of business going against its own best interests, and not the sole doing of schemers and manipulators in the Pentagon and the State Department. To a large extent, business had lost sight of the imperatives of money and abandoned its traditional money-inspired criticism of military intervention and war. By 1953, 13.5 percent of the gross national product was going to defense, up from 5.2 percent in 1950; budget deficits began to appear, $4 billion in fiscal 1951-52 and $9.5 billion for 1952-53. More ominously, inflation also reared its unfashionable head.

The domino theory and other geopolitical rationales offered for the military expeditions in Korea, Central America, and Indochina convinced almost no one in the general population. Paul Johnson says of the Korean War and of the popular reaction to it: "The Korean War was a characteristic 20th-century tragedy. It was launched for ideological reasons, without a scintilla of moral justification or any evidence of popular support." This is borne out by the polls: at the end of World War II, 87 percent of the American people approved of President Truman, but by November of 1951, only 23 percent liked what he was doing.[9] In fact, what was at stake had nothing to do with Korea itself, but rather with the ongoing war on the money front. The testimony of E. C. Reid, a former Canadian undersecretary of state, is eloquent: "The United States did not see Korea as strategically important, [Dean] Acheson told [Lester Pearson, Canada's foreign affairs minister at the time of the Korean War]. It was just that the war in Korea made it possible to get a quick increase in defense spending."[10]

However, the unwillingness of the general public to foot the bill for the military buildup (not to mention the aversion to getting killed) was such that Eisenhower, even though he dutifully took up the traditional Republican slogans of total victory over international communism, got elected on a platform of balanced budgets and reduced military spending. Amazingly enough, Eisenhower delivered the goods: by 1955 he had shrunk the defense budget by 20 percent, and in 1956 the budget showed a surplus. Of course, Eisenhower had the great advantage over traditional politicians that he was not impressed by the uniforms and grandiose strategies of his erstwhile fellow brass-hats.

When Kennedy swept into the White House in the early 1960s, he aimed at reviving an economy which was giving every sign of slowing down. He also embarked on the great strategic missile buildup and took decisive steps toward military involvement in Southeast Asia. But there is every indication that even Kennedy and his Camelot idealists did not undertake their military buildup out of economic considerations. "It is far more likely that *at first strategic and later political considerations were primary* and that administration leaders considered the economic impact something of a bonus, an important and welcome side-effect."[11]

From every point of view Vietnam was even more of a catastrophe than Korea. Vietnam was obviously a pointless war; liberals and leftists may have believed that greedy multinational capitalists were using the armed forces to secure access to Vietnam's tin deposits and offshore oil, and some business leaders may have believed that an alliance of Chinese communist surrogates and peace marchers intended to deprive them of those resources, but no one else did. Vietnam was a local war fought with the crusaders' rhetoric and the cost-no-object attitude which are best reserved for global conflicts. Roberts McNamara, then secretary of defense, made it clear that money caution had been thrown to the winds, that the war simply had to be fought no matter what the cost: "The thing we value most deeply is not money, but men."[12] Meanwhile, the most potent criticism of the war revolved around money considerations. These ranged from putting the army's body counts in perspective by calculating the astronomical cost of killing a single Vietcong soldier to the simple realization by potential draftees that the whole mess was awfully detrimental to their career plans. Vietnam was the first war which America fought in open, conscious defiance of money imperatives: national humiliation and endless money woes would be the cost of this foolishness.

The Hidden Costs of Vietnam

Despite their deserved reputation for ruthlessness in business, the original money men, the Morgans, the Edisons, and the Fords, were concerned, critical individuals who judged war from a point of view which was not that of the common people of their days: after all, in the 1890s or even in the 1930s, not many people had a sufficient experience of money to evaluate government policies in terms of money. The generation of business leaders which emerged from World War II were a different breed. With a few exceptions, the larger-than-life, individualistic tycoons had disappeared; the voice of post–World War II business was that of corporations, of institutions; and the reflex of these institutions was to cast in their lot with the biggest corporate institutions of them all, the government and the Pentagon.

American business, having departed from its historical tradition of being critical of military adventurism and having unquestioningly embraced the Vietnam War, shared in the humiliation of the military defeat. The war in Asia dealt a death blow to the myth, born in the post–World War II bomb years, that war is good business.

All the romanticized accounts of innovation in Silicon Valley should not make us forget the hard facts: the high-technology upstarts were hindered because they did not have access to the kind of research and development facilities, not to mention the cash flows, which the large military-oriented corporations had. On the other hand, the latter had to do without some of the best minds around, who refused to have anything to do with anything remotely connected with military work. Both old-line and cutting-edge businesses suffered because of the

war. The Vietnam nightmare and the recession which
followed brought home what had been intuitively understood all along: war is really terrible for business, and
especially for defense contractors because it limits their
ability to make money by nonmilitary work, as Seymour
Melman has shown quite conclusively:

> These companies and their employees no longer had
> the capability to design, manufacture and sell to the
> civilian markets. Long experience in servicing the
> defense agencies of the government under conditions
> where cost had been a secondary matter, resulted in
> a trained incapacity, among many military-industrial
> firms, to operate in a civilian market.[13]

This is unquestionably a major reason for the lacklus-
ter performance of American manufacturers compared
with that of many of their foreign counterparts, like the
Japanese. Not only has a lot off American money been
invested and lost for good in highly questionable military
paraphernalia and expeditions rather than being plowed
back into the more sensible business end of things, but
American industry acquired some of the terrible traits of
money illiteracy characteristic of the military.

Military Reconstruction and Image Building
After Vietnam

The post-Vietnam military has emphasized its role as a
sensible, "equal-opportunity" employer. A major move in
this direction was the switch to a volunteer army accom-
panied with substantial pay increases and guaranteed
training in specialized fields, the military as on-the-job
training for the high-tech society. The new, "be all you
can be" image is that of a military where recruits get
paid to learn how to make money in today's America and
are not ordered to go get killed in somebody else's jungle
or guarding some diplomatic outpost, which is, of course,
exactly the fate which is in store for them.

The military's promise of real career training most often turns out to be nothing more than an empty promise, as the first graduates from the volunteer army are finding out, mainly because "there aren't that many skilled jobs in the services ... defending the nation remains largely a low-tech business. ... In fact when skilled work is required, the military relies on civilian workers and outside contractors every bit as much as on its own personnel."[14]

Simply raising wages and offering new training programs did not exactly transform the public's perception that the military is a losing money proposition. Many parents simply do not want to send their sons and daughters into an institution associated with large-scale waste and incompetence, let alone see them killed because of this incompetence. Parents know that even if their children were to learn computer programming during their stint in the service, they will also acquire habits which have no place in a modern society: unquestioning submission to a rigid hierarchy's arbitrary decisions, and laxity in the implementation of quality standards. As Hodding Carter noted, "the new awakening of patriotism" will mean "billions for defense ... with an implicit footnote: but not my kids."[15] The classic notion of joining the military to earn one's "manhood" has lost its credibility if only because while the notion of adulthood has changed and now includes a large dose of money savvy, the military still clings to its idea of "a few good men."

Defense in the 1980s, or How to Pay Lip Service to Money

The recent round of superficial exposés uncovering defense cost overruns large and small, collusion between Pentagon officials and defense contractors, and prematurely obsolete weapons systems is little more than the Pentagon putting on a show for the benefit of an increasingly concerned (and taxed) public, demonstrating that is willing to try to become more businesslike, responding to those critics who insist that it should be at least as efficient as IBM, which manages to run a huge disciplined organization and balance its books at the same time. *The New York Times*, for instance, regularly argues that the military should conform to the standard business ethics:

> There seems to be a growing consensus that the way the Defense Department customarily does business is based on an inverted system of rewards and punishments. . . . These incentives tend to reward rather than penalize cost increases in a tank or airplane. . . . The Department of Defense stands the way we normally buy things on its head.[16]

The Pentagon needs to keep a certain level of credibility as a business partner because it simply doesn't have the expertise to develop and maintain the sophisticated weapons systems it is so fond of. What makes America's military-industrial complex palatable is its industrial component. Should business fully accept the incompatibility between sound money practice and military imperatives, and gather the nerve to dissociate itself from the agendas set up by the defense agencies, the military would finally be stripped of its image as an inefficient but basically benevolent distributor of lucrative business contracts and a decent conduit for political patronage by way of the maintaining of often redundant local military bases. To counter this, a new kind of military reformer is emerging, who is trying to chart the course for the military in the coming years by emphasizing rather than downplaying the fundamental differences between the world of money and that of the military, with an eye toward freeing the latter from the moderating influence of money.

The Military in the 1990s and Beyond: Desperately Trying to Escape from the Constraints of Money

One way around the issue of the military's lack of money intelligence is to say that defense serves a higher master than the mighty dollar and that by definition it must be judged by other criteria. One of the foremost proponents of this position is Edward Luttwak, a prominent theorist of modern warfare, who unbendingly defends the right and duty of the military to defy the classic "materialist" logic of the market where efficiency, and more specifically cost efficiency, is the ultimate measure of achievement:

> In searching for mismanagement and waste, we naturally compare what the Pentagon is doing with commonsense civilian notions of efficiency. This seems reasonable; after all, efficiency measures output against effort, and inefficiency can scarcely be a Good Thing. The trouble is the outputs that count in war are very particular and very different from the outputs that count in peacetime, and when civilian notions of efficiency are applied, the difference is routinely overlooked.[17]

There is certainly a lot of truth to this; the military's function is quite different from that of any normal business. The latter must eventually show a plus in the profit column if it is to survive, while the function of the military, according to their job description, is not to make money but to spend it.

> After all, the everyday business of the Army, Navy, Marine Corps, and Air Force, of their civilian secretariats, and of the Defense Department civilians is not to wage war or mount commando raids, but rather to recruit and train manpower, both military and civilian, commissioned and enlisted; to select,

purchase, and assimilate new arms and equipment; to research and develop future weapons and all that goes with them; to repair and supply equipment and training to lesser allies; and finally to engage in the deployment, exercise, and routine operation of combat and ancillary forces, both in full-time active units and in part-time reserves, both nuclear and not, home based and overseas.[18]

Wherever he turns, Luttwak discovers that, much to his chagrin, an entire generation of well-intentioned but misguided reformers has contaminated the military with too much of the materialism of the private sector. Therefore, he would like to put as much distance as possible between his brand of army and that which we have known to this day; his obsession is to put as many distinctions as possible between the properly military way of doing things and that of business, which is too efficiency-and cost-conscious and too methodical, too patient. The message is to call the military back to arms, away from the constraints imposed by money. As he puts it, "The military must emphasize surprise and the breaking of routine over methodical, efficient activity":

Consider surprise. How is it achieved? by deception—unless the enemy is merely apathetic or unobservant, and therefore outclassed to begin with. And how is deception achieved? By doing the unexpected. And what is the unexpected? Something other than the sensible, normal and efficient.[19]

In his attempt to put the military beyond the classic cost-benefit analysis, Luttwak is reminiscent of the entrepreneurial cultists and the management gurus; he aims at nothing less than the definition of the soul of a new war machine:

... when it comes to military power, the relationship between material inputs and desired outputs is not proportional; it is in fact very loose, because the making of military strength is dominated by nonmaterial, quite intangible human factors, from the quality of national military strategy to the fighting morale of individual servicemen.[20]

The boys over at *In Search of Excellence, Inc.* couldn't have said it better. What counts is not simply your budget for plant or equipment but also the intellectual and morale resources at your disposal. Luttwak's list of desirable intangibles is very similar to the *current* list of desirable corporate traits. They include: coupling a strong corporate culture ("everyone takes the same risks") with the necessary amount of individual eccentricity and initiative ("brave men are often unconventional in their behavior"); emphasizing strategic planning (the "art of war"); loyalty based on a real rather than abstract liking of the organization resulting from adequate recognition of one's efforts and dedication by the group's leaders ("individual morale").

Suggestions like Luttwak's abound and are gathering support both in and out of the services themselves. They are far from innocuous and their implementation can only lead to the more frequent and more intense use of armed force, since an above-money military would be ideally suited for the purely political wars and skirmishes which have a way of cropping up every six months or so. These engagements are totally devoid of any semblance of economic justification and often make no sense whatsoever even in purely strategic terms; the only reason for them is the need for politicians to reassure themselves and their followers that even though their economic achievements are utterly dismal, they can still control something, namely, the army. Even assuming that threatening the invasion of Cuba over the presence of Russian strategic missiles could be justified as a response to a military threat, one is bound to admit that the more recent uses of the military, actual or threatened, make no more sense from a traditional military point of view than from the perspective of a cost-benefit analysis. The aim of the current crop of military reformers is to put the military beyond both these criteria.

The Nuclear Era and the Myth of Limited War

The balance of terror, military preparedness and determination, diplomatic restraint, the calming influence of peace forums such as the United Nations, have all been credited with preventing the outbreak of global war for the last forty years. But once again, the real peacemonger is money. Nuclear weapons brought a whole new dimension to the cost of waging war. That World War III has not yet happened is not due to a lack of determination to fight it, but to the simple fact that no one can afford to pay for it: the butcher's bill would be prohibitive; no one has the resources to rebuild the world from scratch. Before the atomic age, wars had merely threatened to strain the finance of any nation; any government foolish enough to risk bankruptcy could declare a war which could escalate into a global conflict simply to get out of its foreign or domestic difficulties. But after Hiroshima, it was clear that the cost of nuclear devastation made fighting an all-out war simply unthinkable, even for the richest and the most powerful countries.

Since 1945, military strategists, threatened with unemployment because of the revolution in military thinking brought about by nuclear weapons, have sought a way to make war affordable again by introducing such outlandish notions as limited war and flexible response. Frustrated by the impossibility of fighting the big one, and exhausted by the intellectual effort required by endless war games and think tanks, the world's military has, since 1945, capitalized on every improbable *casus belli*, from Korea to the Falkland Islands, from the Congo to Afghanistan, to start the shooting, or at least to make a show of force, with the terrible result that there have been almost eighty wars declared since 1946, at an average cost of 40,000 casualties a month. These 19 million deaths, roughly equal to the total number of deaths during World War II, are a stern reminder that in the modern world, wars, which are reassuringly dubbed "limited," are anything but limited, and that the military still manages to satisfy at least some of its traditional appetite for war and destruction even when it is kept on a short leash.[21] The idea of lengthening the leash is positively frightening.

Money at Work Behind the Iron Curtain: The Russian War Machine and Its Checking Account

In Russia there is no discussion of the military-industrial complex. Russia *is* a military-industrial complex; such is the avowed purpose of that society. But even in such a context the moderating influence of money is crucial in controlling the growth of the war machine, since the Russian system is under the same kind of obligations as its Western counterparts to deliver benefits to the civilian population, even if the expectations it has to meet are kept at a very low level. The deal struck between the Russian government and its citizenry is that the people will accept great sacrifices which will allow the channeling of the nation's resources into building the most formidable military machine in the world, the one with the most massive rockets, tanks, and space stations. A standard of living equivalent to what it was in the West fifty years ago is promoted as preferable to serfdom and devastation of the country by the Nazis. The government's end of the bargain is that it will not let the standard of living degrade too badly and will periodically make an effort to improve it, however marginally. The government simply cannot totally ignore the Russian citizens' insistence that they get their share of the wealth of the country. The Russian people's cry for money, not the military pressure which the West brings to bear on the Soviet military, is what limits Russian military expenditures.

Soviet officials link their desire to reach new arms agreements with their need to funnel more money into solving economic problems. . . . "We need much more money for the development of the economy," says Lev Seymeko, an arms-control specialist at the influential [Russian] United States and Canada Institutes. . . . "We need a revolution of our economy and that takes investment. If we have to engage in an arms race, it will delay the level of development of our society."[22]

Toward Money Literacy: Doubts Within the Military-Industrial Complex

Almost half a century after World War II, many people, finally coming to their money senses, are reaching the conclusion arrived at by Seymour Melman twenty years ago, that "a permanent war economy . . . has the traceable effect of generating uninvestable capital and unemployable labor, even though the immediately visible consequence of military spending is employing people to do that work."[23] This has become obvious enough that such a major defense contractor as Rockwell International is now reluctant to put all its eggs in the Pentagon basket, as indicated in the recent *Business Week* headline[24] "Rockwell Using Its Cash Hoard to Move Away from Defense." Similarly, some of the largest chemical companies are wary of engaging in the seemingly lucrative development of the next generation of chemical weapons because:

> The nerve agent business holds little promise of long-running revenues, because after the military stockpiles have been topped off the production plants will be geared down to a state of readiness. . . . Some companies say the program did not suit their corporate strategy. "It's just not our niche," said Monsanto company vice president John F. Hussey. "Generally the military contracting business is not a place that Monsanto believes is in the best interest of its share-

holders in the years ahead." Union Carbide told the
Pentagon that nerve gas was "not in keeping with
our overall production and marketing strategy. . . ."
The industry view was clearly colored by a fear of
bad press and liability.[25]

The high-technology industries have long been seen as
totally dependent on defense contracts, and it has been
argued that the economic fallouts of such schemes as the
Strategic Defense Initiative would give America's technology a needed shot in the arm, but even traditionally
moderate forces take the opposite view:

> America's main advantages in high-tech industries
> do not come from defense spending. . . . America
> chiefly gets its punch from its huge internal market,
> from its entrepreneurial exuberance. . . . A big star-
> wars program could end up wastefully draining scarce
> engineering talent away from commercial enterprise.
> Ask any American electronics executive today what
> benefits Star Wars will likely bring to the industry; a
> blank stare is the likely response.[26]

The inescapable problem with defense spending is that
it is a self-contained system, an end in itself:

> Its products do not yield ordinary economic use-value:
> usefulness for the level of living (consumer goods and
> services); or usefulness for further production (as in
> machinery or tools being used to make other arti-
> cles). . . . Ordinarily a civilian economy can look for-
> ward to making substantial advances in its total
> productivity because of the gains that can be made
> in the efficiency of machines and in the efficiency of
> labor. . . . However if new machinery, however effi-
> cient, is installed for producing military materiel,
> then what emerges is military materiel which no
> factory can use for any further production. The result
> is that the normally available addition to production
> capability which stems from installing new produc-

tion equipment is forgone for the whole society. . . .
Similar reasoning applies to the productivity of labor. . . . When the investment in fresh educational
competence, at whatever level, is subsequently applied to nonproductive (defense) economic activity,
then the community loses the potential economic gain
from human competence that ordinarily accrues to it
when that capability is applied to productive work.[27]

The Military Wants to Put More Underground Than Just Missiles

Today more than ever, money and its levelheaded, cost-
conscious logic contribute to the containment of military
spending and adventurism around the world. Wherever it
turns, the military finds itself the target of money-inspired
criticism, either because of its questionable business practices or because of its monopolizing too large a share of
its country's resources, financial and otherwise. The military's response to this criticism never satisfies anybody,
and only encourages the public to take an ever dimmer
view of things military. Hence the tendency of a new
generation of military leaders and strategists to put themselves beyond the range of their critics. Their reflex is to
dive into their bunkers, batten down the hatches, and
forget about the outside world. Retrenchment to the essence of military activity is the order of the day, and
today the essence of military activity is the weird world
of the expanding and Byzantine system of intelligence
and security clearances, war rooms, war games, and endless contingency plans. Those people in the general staffs
and command centers and crisis cabinets are not hiding
from terrorists or from foreign missiles as much as from
the limits imposed on them by the preoccupation of normal folks with the cost of war and war preparations.

The Inadequacy of the Peace Movement

The military is probably not overly worried about the various nuclear disarmament campaigns; it may even be quite pleased with them. Once nuclear weapons are abolished, part of the money restraint on the activities of the military will be removed, and war would be brought one huge step closer to affordability. Moral criticism of the military, such as that voiced in the various nuclear disarmament campaigns, will be easily satisfied, as the strategists give up on nuclear wapons, which they cannot use anyway. Like a thief who drops the wallet he took from you just as he is about to be caught, hoping that you will stop running after him, the modern military has already begun to jettison its nuclear arsenal, physical and theoretical, in favor of a return to conventional war, which this time around will be executed with the efficiency, accuracy, and awesome power of the new "smart," nonnuclear weapons systems developed by defense contractors in departments shielded from the scrutiny of auditors and shareholders in the name of national security. The chances for continuing peace rest on preventing the world's military from developing into autonomous entities oblivious to money's scrutiny and control. Making money and insisting it be used intelligently is not a cowardly concession to power politics or a selfish retreat from the "real issues," but the only way to instill some sanity into the strange, volatile, and dangerous universe of strategists and geopoliticians.

─────Money Myth 5:─────
The Business of America Is Business

THE MYTH: Business, a loosely defined assortment of activities aimed at producing, selling, and financing goods and services, is the very foundation of the American way of life. America owes its greatness to its unique ability to turn out quality products and to offer innovative services. The history of the continent's development is the history of business. America's interests are best served by turning the priorities of business, such as competition, productivity, and access to cheap sources of energy, raw materials, and labor, into national policy.

The Myth in Action

The pervasive notion that the business of America is business has contributed more than anything else to the general confusion which seems to characterize any discussion of the future of the world's economy. The future of America's trade relations, be it with the other developed countries, notably Japan and Canada, or with the developing countries, is always considered in terms of the trade deficit which threatens the United States' traditional manufacturing sector. Any new perspective on a new international order is overshadowed by the paranoid

notion that America will somehow dissolve if its traditional businesses should disappear from the scene. We
are confronted with the endless repetition of the idea that
the best way for the nation as a whole and for individuals
to make money is to return to the basics of business,
which generally means the basics of industrial production.
Many Americans even look to Japan for a clue to the
future, not realizing that Japan is, *mutatis mutandis*, at
the stage which the United States reached thirty years
ago.

Attempts to make the imperatives of business the imperatives of national policy are always disastrous, because sooner or later they evolve into protectionism, the
definition of spheres of influence and the like. We need to
take a look at history in order to realize that business
was never the root business of America; in fact, business
is not even the real business of business.

The Myth Unraveled: The Business of Business Is Not Business

Some of us can remember our grandfathers reading
Business Week in the 1950s. In those days the magazine
was a rather forbidding affair, its cover mostly done in
shades of sepia brown; it was, in every sense of the word,
strictly business. One only has to pick up a current issue
of today's *Business Week* to see how business, its public
image, and its preoccupations have changed; not only
has the magazine become a slick glossy with mass circulation, but its contents are evidence that business is neither the sole nor even the main preoccupation of today's
business people. The better part of the magazine is devoted to the discussion of politics, marketing, and, most
of all, investment strategies and other issues more directly related to money itself than to the practice of
business. Not only *Business Week* but the business press
at large reflects a dramatic change in emphasis: the world
is seen less as the universe of business, where the refer-

ence point is the production and circulation of goods and services, and increasingly as that of money, where money itself is the way to get rich. There is more and more coverage of the actions of the Federal Reserve Board, the Securities and Exchange Commission, and the trends of international banking, Eurodollar markets, and foreign debt problems, since this is clearly what matters in today's world, where business people themselves are usually much more concerned with money, under the guise of finance, foreign exchange, or the proper utilization of profits, than with the particulars of their specific business.

Today most companies have come to the same conclusion reached years ago at General Motors, when it proclaimed that it was in the business of making money, not cars. Coming to terms with money, and with the idea that one's main business is to make money, is much more difficult than mastering industrial processes, acquiring technical expertise, and developing a winning marketing strategy. Even the most sophisticated production process is, in the end, quite concrete; matter is transformed, the end product can generally be seen going somewhere, its characteristics and behavior are more or less predictable. The same goes for services: very concrete and tangible dirt is removed from buildings, streets, and polluted waters, transportation companies move physical persons and objects over measurable distances at more or less predictable times, computer services companies process data and generate up with printouts, mailing lists, and the like. But money itself is abstract. Modern money is not something physical; it can hardly be touched, it seems always to be in transit over some phone line or some other kind of data link; unlike a product or a service, money is not predictable; it is possible with some patience to understand "whence it came and where it went," but it is another thing altogether to understand where it's going. This is why the realization that one is in the business of making money and not in the business of supplying some defined product or service is often shattering and disquieting.

Books like *In Search of Excellence* probably owe their

popularity not so much to their originality, but to their basically nostalgic outlook: they offer the promise of a straight, no-nonsense business environment; they make a good show of bucking the trend toward acknowledging money's central role, of calling businesses back to the brass tacks of production, to the reassuring world of responding to customers' needs and taking reasonably good care of the work force. Many preachers of "excellence" and of "industrial policy" think of themselves as crusaders whose sacred mission is to remind General Motors that it is in the business of making cars, not money. The problem with this approach is that it requires the remarkable leap of faith of believing that Nissan, Honda, or Toyota is not in the business of making money.

Americans, Business, and Money

The special place of money in America has not failed to affect individual attitudes, as individual Americans become more and more convinced that they are, much like business, essentially in the business of making money, and not in the business of working. As a result, Americans identify much less with business than do Europeans or Japanese. In Europe or Japan, people have great faith in business, especially in whatever business employs them. In America the era of the Organization Man was reminiscent of this way of life where the business one works for is the guarantee of a decent life: the company gave you a job with a future, and as the company kept on expanding you got either a pay increase or a promotion, or a combination of the two. This system is now all but extinct. In today's uniquely flexible American employment system, just about anyone can be laid off without the long advance notices and prolonged severance payments which are mandatory in most of Europe, and without the guarantee of continuing employment somewhere else in the company, as is the norm in Japan. In such an environment, people rely on whatever money they have rather than on the wisdom, foresight, and benevolence of the business which employs them. They see whatever money they manage to save, beg, steal, or otherwise accumulate as their best for survival, while they expect relatively little from business or government.

The Business of America Has Never Been Business

The current preoccupation with money is simply due to the rediscovery of a very basic truth: the real business of America has never been business, but money. Throughout history the uniqueness of America has always been expressed, not by America's way of doing business, but by its handling of money matters. Americans around 1776 were involved in pretty much the same pre–Industrial Revolution businesses as any other people around the world: trading, mostly in the products of agriculture in a more or less colonial mercantilist context, and early experiments in manufacture and basic engineering. But what set the Americans apart, as early as the 1690s, was their money ingenuity, their readiness to experiment with new forms of money.

It is vital to realize that, for all their agricultural resources and their trading activity, the British colonies of North America faced a serious shortage of money. The dominant form of money, essential for foreign trade, consisted of hard money, under the specific form of specie, coined money. But unlike the Spanish colonies in Mexico and South America, they had neither gold nor silver mines; California and the Klondike simply did not exist at the time. The great historian of early American banking, Bray Hammond, offers a vivid description of this predicament, insisting on "the basic fact ... that the 18th century Americans, being without specie to serve as a medium of exchange and legal tender, had to provide something."[1] In fact, the lack of precious metals was such that the colonies of Virginia and Maryland used tobacco

as legal tender; according to Galbraith, "the use of tobacco as money survived in Virginia for nearly two centuries and in Maryland for a century and a half." Of
course, as has been pointed out, notably by Galbraith,
the lack of precious metals had been overcome by other
bullion-deprived traders, for instance the Venetians: the
trick is to sell your wares for gold and silver.[2] But this
would have been a rather slow process, especially in view
of the mercantilist bent of the British colonial trading
system; it would have taken centuries for America to
accumulate enough hard money to sustain the rapid development of its huge territory.

In the Beginning There Was Money

This is why, very early on, America turned to paper
money. This is not remarkable per se; various experiments with paper money, usually in the guise of bank
notes, had been taking place for some time in many parts
of the world. What was unique was that in America,
paper money actually worked and supported real prosperity, instead of producing the wild speculation, scandals, political crises, and massive bankruptices associated
with the European attempts at using paper money. Hammond describes how in the 1750s the Rhode Island col-
ony was flourishing under a regime of paper money, at
the very time when paper money was viewed with utter
suspicion in most countries, notably in France. Inciden-
tally, it is worth noting that, as is so often the case,
money and freedom went hand in hand; Rhode Island
was considered "a haven for refugees from the theocra-
cies of Massachusetts and Connecticut and a pioneer of
religious and political tolerance."[3]

In this context it is not surprising that money was
at the core of the discontent of the American colonies
toward England. In Galbraith's words, "differences of view
over issuing money were an important cause of friction"
in the relations between London and its colonies. In the

eyes of the colonial power in London, paper money was a tool of emanicipation; colonies like Rhode Island were so successful at using it that in 1751 " [the English] Parliament forbade the issue of further paper money in New England and thirteen years later extended the ban to the rest of the colonies. A tactless exception was made for paper issued for the King's purposes, that is to say for war."[4]

America's early familiarity with the new form of money was to prove crucial to the achievement of independence when the Continental Congress found itself desperately short of the hard money needed for the purpose of outfitting, feeding, and paying the republican troops. The problem was especially pressing since the Congress had no powers of taxation. Franklin, Jefferson, Washington, and Paine may have made great contributions to the development of electricity, printing, philosophy, agriculture, military strategy, and the art of chopping cherry trees, but their greatest, most innovative accomplishment was the creation on very short notice of a suitably versatile, yet sufficiently trustworthy, kind of money, the Continental Note, which offered a solution to the money woes of the Congress. That Continental Notes gained acceptance in spite of the persistent doubts about paper money in a land dominated by farmers is indicative of the level of money sophistication of early America; in many other places the bid for independence would probably have failed simply because people would have insisted on being paid in hard specie. Paper money was so crucial to the success of the American Revolution that, says Galbraith, "Beside the Liberty Bell there might well be a tasteful replica of a Continental Note."[5]

Money and the Constitution

After the War of Independence, money was a central issue in the debates of the Constitutional Convention. The early and successful uses of paper money in the erstwhile colonies, culminating in the undeniable success of the Continental Notes in financing the war, had made most of the delegates, men brought up in the British tradition of hard money, very uneasy; they were having second thoughts; maybe the genie should, after all, be put back into the bottle. In the words of a delegate, "One gigantic speculation had been notably successful—the achieving of independence." The backlash was soon felt. When the convention began to formulate the monetary clauses of the Consitution, says Hammond, "The aim was, in the words of various delegates, 'to shut and bar the door against paper money.' "[6]

For all the reluctance of the delegates, monetary innovation was nevertheless the order of the day. The young nation was still perilously short of hard money: estimates of the amount of specie in the colonies before independence range from $8 million to $12 million, hardly enough to support life, liberty, and the pursuit of happiness in any context other than strict Jeffersonian rusticity. Moreover, America did not have a banking system. Something had to be done and, ultimately, a compromise was reached. The Convention ruled that the states would be prohibited from granting bank charters, while the central government was forbidden to issue paper money.

Despite the political hesitations, the nation's need for money was such that the development of the monetary system went ahead rapidly and, on the whole, quite successfully. According to Hammond, "When the Bank of England was a century old, in 1794, there were but four chartered banks in the British Isles. There were then already eighteen chartered banks in America, only thirteen years after incorporation of the first American bank." This number more than quadrupled over the following decade, to seventy-five in 1805. And, surprisingly enough for a banking system which, unlike Europe's, had not emerged from centuries of capital accumulation and experimentation, there were no bank failures until 1809, a testimony of the flexibility, resilience, and perceived trustworthiness of the fledgling banks.[7]

Since the federal government was prohibited from printing money, the existence and circulation of paper money depended on the issuing, circulation, and acceptance as legal tender of bank notes. The Americans had improved on the European banking tradition going all the way back to the Medicis and before, and developed a financial system every bit as efficient as that of the then-one-hundred-year-old Bank of England.

The young Republic's money institutions played no small part in determining its political character at a time when it was unclear whether the new country would veer toward democracy or a form of aristocratic oligarchy. "According to Noah Webster both public debt and banks were instruments of mercantile triumph over the survival of feudalism, and it was for such reasons that Thomas Paine advocated them." In those days usury, the financial version of feudalism, if allowed to proliferate, could well have seriously jeopardized the development of the young nation by making funds scarce and expensive; the result would probably have been a paralysis of industrial and commercial development and the appearance in its place of a kind of postcolonial landed aristocracy which would have totally dominated the social landscape. A major function of the early banking system was to control usury. In fact, "the usurers 'never intermitted in their efforts to destroy the bank.' "[8]

The early success of America in monetary matters was due to acts of financial daring closely paralleling the acts of political courage which had led to the Declaration of Independence. One is hard put to find a better expression than Hammond's: "The Americans had declared their political independence before it was a reality, not after; and what they did in the matter of financial competence was much the same."[9] The gamble soon paid off; money was soon established on a footing solid enough to contribute mightily to the development of a continent which was just beginning to be discovered.

Early Development and Settlement

From the very beginning, America's uniquely flexible and decentralized banking system was the key to its development, because it ensured that there was always enough money in the right places and in the right pockets at the right time. This involved attracting and managing foreign money, since at the time, "London was the world money market . . . and America, like any underdeveloped country, had to import capital to grow." The most vital business of America during those years of settlement and original development was not building railroads and canals, tilling the land or opening foundries and steel mills, but putting capital, mostly foreign capital invested in American banks or ventures, to good use. America may have been the land of freedom and opportunity for the immigrants, but it was even more so for the money which the rest of the world was enthusiastically investing in America. The result was that by 1809 the Bank of the United States alone had capital amounting to $10 million, $8.5 million in deposits, and $4.5 million worth of bank notes in circulation. Obviously, this was a major change from the prerevolutionary days of scarce money.[10]

It can even be said that America, by attracting capital, saved Europe from suffering more self-destruction than it did in the course of the nineteenth-century wars, for the simple reason that the money invested in America was not available for waging war. The mind boggles at the thought of what massacres Napoleon would have carried out had he had access to greater financial resources than he had. The case of Stephen Girard is probably typical of many who pulled their money out of Europe, as Hammond relates, "in alarm at the way Bonaparte's empire was expanding." Girard withdrew some $1 million from Europe, first to Britain, then to America; eventually he used about $400,000 of this to take over the Philadelphia operations of the Bank of the United States when its charter was not renewed.[11] Any money which crossed the Atlantic in the other direction, such as the money paid out to Napoleon for the purchase of Louisiana, was most likely to be used for destructive purposes.

The results were astonishing; America was discovering itself, making the transition from mercantilism to enterprise. In the words of Hammond, "In 1791 American business had been concerned with foreign commerce; by 1816 it was concerned with a greatly diversified internal economy." He adds, "Bank credit was to America a new source of energy, like steam. . . ."[12] The changes were soon reflected in the geography of the country. Philadelphia, the great center of mercantilist wealth, had also been the center of government and banking. Now government was moving to its own, purpose-built city, Washington. And while wealth may have remained in old Philadelphia, money was quickly moving to Manhattan's Wall Street.

Meanwhile, court cases and legislative actions concerning money and banking multiplied, revealing what Hammond describes as "the mesh of moral, economic and constitutional problems which were profoundly disturbing to the American people." Beyond the individual business ventures and specific transformations of the landscape of the social fabric, "The coventions of a monetary economy were coming swiftly into use and sweeping the unsophisticated off their feet. . . . These devices yielded fortunes and so had validity, but they were as unsettling to society as were in their way the Newtonian physics, the sentiments of the French Revolution, romanticism, or machinery driven by steam." There was a basic difference, however, between monetary and technological or political innovation. Political reformers had a fairly good idea of the systems of government they wanted and of how to go about setting them up. Similarly, an inventor like Fulton had a substantially accurate idea of the physics of steam. But where money was concerned, the innovations were so great that practice was always ahead, not simply of theory, but of the understanding of the very people who were most central to the phenomenon. Hammond's comment is that "I doubt if one banker in four clearly understood what he was doing and what made it sound and proper."[13]

The Reaction Against Money: Agrarians, Frontiersmen, and Slave Masters

The changes wrought by money, if they were difficult to grasp for the people involved in banking, were incomprehensible, disturbing, and threatening to others, notably to farmers and to the mass of immigrants, who came from places where money had nothing like the velocity and the volatility which it was acquiring in America. People like John Jacob Astor were getting incredibly rich not so much because they had innovative business ideas (Astor's original business, fur trading, was as old as the continent; it had been one of the mainstays of the American Indians' economy long before the first Europeans got in on the act some two or three hundred years before Astor), but because they realized that money was a powerful force, that it was something worth paying for; even when he had to pay 30 percent interest rates, Astor still considered that the money he borrowed was his best investment.

But for one Astor who realized that he was in the business of making money, not trading furs, there were thousands who were completely baffled, even horrified, by the complex social environment of the urbanized and rapidly industrializing eastern seaboard. Most perplexing to the new immigrants was that this new environment was held together, not by family ties, by allegiance to a monarch, or even by an overwhelming police force, but by money. For many, ready as they were for a new land, this was a bit much, and it encouraged them to embark on the way out west, where, they hoped, life would be simpler. The widespread perception of the frontier as the embodiment of the most traditional values is well founded. On the whole, far from being bold innovators, those who headed for the frontier were engaged in a nostalgic reaction against the new money-centered life-style of the American Northeast.

Typical of the frontier mentality was the outright prohibition of banking in the original constitutions of the states of Texas, Iowa, and Arkansas. "For more than two hundred years, the 'frontier,' whether colonial or national, was manned by agrarians on the defensive against business enterprise and especially against banks, once they were introduced." The result was that "the agrarians, with characteristic love of stability, forbade banking because it was a source of instability." Their feeling was that "in a democracy of plain, honest folk, the only proper money—the only money permitted by the Constitution—wsa silver and gold, whose worth was known and whose volume, like that of rain from heaven, was determined for the inscrutable good of man by an all-wise, benevolent Providence."[14] This seemed to be confirmed in the late 1840s when it appeared that at the end of the trail lay the gold mines of California and Oregon: there was a real pot of gold, of hard money, at the end of the agrarian rainbow, the promise of freedom from the complexities of modern money.

Of course, the South was even more estranged from the money mainstream than the West. The southerners stood not merely for agrarianism but for slavery, in effect enslaving themselves to a chronic lack of money, Since the slaves, by definition, did not have access to money, the South was essentially without the broad consumer base necessary for the diversified production of goods and services. Worse, the slave owners' stubborn resistance to money posed a serious threat to the expansion of money in the North and precipitated the tragic war between the states.

Another dark chapter of American history should be reexamined: the near extermination of the Indians. It must be stressed that the moving force behind this genocide was not some conspiracy of greedy easterners, but the frenzied flight from money by settlers seeking a simpler, moneyless existence who undertook, with government approval, the outright expropriation of the natives' land. The Wild West was exactly that: wilderness, the absence of money or of any elementary economic consideration. The eastern industrialists always paid some kind of wage to their employees; the southern slave drivers at least fed their slaves, however badly; but the settlers simply shot the Indians.

The consequences of the original land grabbers' anti-money attitudes are still with us, as witnessed by the current financial troubles afflicting American farmers. These are, it is to be hoped, the last stage in what Bray Hammond, speaking of the very beginnings of the country, described as the "slow realization that farming must be a means of making money, not of withholding oneself from the world."[15]

Money and Industry

During the late nineteenth and early twentieth century period of industrialization, American industry may have become famous because of its efficient management systems and its technological innovations, but here again its one outstanding characteristic was its unequaled effficiency at chaneling investments where needed, its unique ability not only to make money but to make money circulate. J. P. Morgan's claim to fame was not that he ran a railroad, no matter how great a railroad it may have been, but that he managed to set up the first billion-dollar company. Edison did not get all the recognition he did because he invented incandescent lighting, but because he was the first to make a fortune selling light bulbs.

That money is the key to business and not vice versa is clearly shown today by the increased autonomy and clout of the financial department in most corporations, after years of dominance by the engineering, marketing, and legal departments. And it is only normal that this shift should occur as industries and corporations reach maturity. In a way, businesses are not greatly different from individuals. In their childhood most people are unaware of money; during their adolescence they tend to consider money as a reward for a job well done; only when they reach adulthood do they realize that money is their life-blood, the most important concern of their lives. In its infancy a business, often privately held, often with little or no money, develops a product, then, in adolescence, concentrates on its core business, struggles in the marketplace, and is rewarded by handsome profits. In time the business finally reaches maturity: it not only makes money but spends more and more time managing its money, often "going public"; on the stock exchange the fate of companies hinges on their perceived ability to make money, not on the excellence of their products or services. Even privately held businesses, and the wealth of the individuals who control them, are for all practical purposes evaluated as if their shares were publicly traded.

World War II: A Victory Misunderstood

The most startling result of World War II was that, in the words of Martin Mayer, "The war ended with virtually all the world's gold in the United States, and no reason to believe it would ever leave."[16] If this had been a seventeenth-century war, this would have been total victory and then some: all the booty had been captured. A young country which, less than two centuries before, started with practically no hard money now had enough bullion to put to shame not only France, Germany, and Japan but imperial Britain herself.

Of course, this vital aspect of the victory was not easily perceptible by the population at large; rather, the victory was seen as the triumph of American industrial might, of American business. This led America to think of itself as an industrial power whose purpose was to compete with the businesses of other countries and whose national interest was to secure access to cheap sources of raw materials. This emphasis on business overshadowed the more important and even more overwhelming victory of America on the money front.

The ambivalence of victory led to an ambivalence in the behavior of postwar America, and ultimately to the current rampant American identity crisis. On one hand,

America had to get money moving again in the postwar world; but on the other, America was thinking in terms of geopolitical imperatives.

At the end of the war the ravaged nations of Europe and Asia were not crying for revenge, they were crying for money in order to heal their wounds. This cry had a special urgency because America and money, on top of their military victory, had won the hearts and minds of people the world over. People everywhere had been exposed to American money behavior, if only through coming in contact with the G.I.'s: never before had an army on the march had so much money. Even more important, the American soldiers, from private to general, simply took money for granted; this immensely powerful army and its well-fed personnel could not be bothered with looting and plundering; what they wanted was to buy things. In the postwar years, not only was the world deprived of money while America was richer than ever, but America and Americans, by their very behavior, were creating a pressing demand for money. Hence the special responsibility of America to play a major, and if necessary innovative, role in the world's money affairs.

The goal of the Bretton Woods Conference, held in July 1944, had been to solve the problem of getting money moving again in the postwar environment. The conference's success in elaborating an acceptable and workable international monetary system is generally attributed to the brilliant theories of John Maynard Keynes; however, it was America which had the most crucial role in the practical implementation of the Bretton Woods agreements, since the new international monetary system basically relied on the dollar as its reserve currency. From the start, it was clear that the two creations of Bretton Woods, the World Bank and the International Monetary Fund, basically expressed and depended on the United States' money wisdom (or lack thereof).

America's taking charge of the world's money was not limited to the multilateral agreements of Bretton Woods. The United States went ahead with its own initiatives for the reconstruction of the war-torn world. The Marshall

Plan was not only something unheard-of on the part of a victorious power; it also made a much greater contribution to repairing the damage of war than did the International Monetary Fund. The IMF's resources were a scant $6.8 billion, while the Marshall Plan appropriations totaled $12.5 billion.[17] This was America at its best, more than meeting the expectations of a world which looked up to it for money sense.

The other side of the coin was that in other respects America began to behave like a classic "world power," complete with spheres of influence, and lines of supply in need of military protection. As a consequence, at the same time when the whole world was growing ever more confident about America's sense of monetary responsibility, there appeared the first misgivings about America's motives, even among America's allies. There is a strong indication that in the eyes of Canada and the European nations which joined NATO, "The purpose of the North Atlantic Treaty Organization was not just to contain or restrain the Soviet Union; it was to contain or restrain the United States."[18] At the end of World War I, Woodrow Wilson was considered by every nation as the bringer of peace. Now Americans were considered, even by their allies, as potential warmongers. America was quickly becoming schizophrenic, torn between its money responsibilities and the geopolitical ambitions of some of its ruling elite.

Toward Money Literacy: The Aftermath of Vietnam

Much has been said about Vietnam being the expression of America's identity crisis, but there is a lot of confusion as to the nature of this crisis. Vietnam was essentially the explosion of the myth that the business of America is business. Without a doubt the war was good for business: military contracts provided steady work and rising profits; and because government depended so

much on the cooperation of business, it was more responsive than ever to the pressures of the various business
lobbies. What domestic support there was for the war
rested on the notion that the war was good for business
and that what is good for business is good for the country
(i.e., in the no-nonsense terms of American democracy,
good for the individual citizen's money). But the war was
being fought in defiance of money common sense. Without simplifying too much, it is fair to say that rather
than raising taxes in order to finance the war, the United
States government chose to print money instead. This
was only possible because the world had confidence in
America's outstanding record of money wisdom since 1945:
it seemed unthinkable that America would do something
as outrageous and devious as resorting to the printing
press to finance a war. When the truth became known,
the impact was great both on the nation's psyche and on
America's image abroad; the feeling was that the United
States had betrayed the world's trust in its money sense.
As Martin Mayer pointed out more than ten years ago:
"The loss of faith in American idealism . . . should be
seen not as a result of revisionist history or Asian war but
as a natural reaction to the betrayal of the trust America
accepted—not knowing very much about what it was
doing—in the late 1940s."[19]

The long and difficult period of inflation and recession,
which was a direct consequence of the money-be-damned
approach to financing the war in Asia, was a stern reminder to Americans that the business of America is not
business, and that claims to the effect should be viewed
with the utmost suspicion because too many businesses
are little more than privately owned branches of the
government.

Money and the Constitutional Balance of Power in the 1980s

The dreadful consequences of the war lingered on. For almost ten years after the troops had pulled out of Saigon, life seemed a succession of worsening inflation, deficits, and industrial failures, ultimately turning into the worst recession since the 1930s. Against this dreary background, the Federal Reserve Board under the leadership of Paul A. Volcker managed to emerge as a powerful shaper of national policy. This is a somewhat remarkable development. In 1975 John Kenneth Galbraith could describe the Board as "a place of deposit not alone for public funds but also for men who could not reliably be trusted to balance their own checkbooks." Now, little more than a decade later, the Fed is widely perceived as the enforcer of money common sense in the politics-government-business nexus. This is more or less unexpected, since, technically, the Fed is something which "belongs" to the executive branch, not unlike the armed services. But there is a big difference: the President, as Commander in Chief, may order the Joint Chiefs of Staff around, but he has no such direct authority over the members of the Federal Reserve Board. Like the justices of the Supreme Court who owe their final allegiance to the Constitution, the governors of the Fed owe theirs to money, something which even they have only recently come to realize.

For all practical purposes, the current balance of power involves a fourth and determining element besides the traditional legislative, executive, and judicial powers: the monetary. Congress, the legislative, represents the interests of business and consumers; the executive embodies reasons of state in matters of policy both foreign and domestic; the judiciary protects the integrity of the Constitution; but it is left to the monetary to keep them all in line with reality, for instance by drawing attention to such follies as the current colossal national debt. In the modern balance of power the monetary is the perpetuator of the great American tradition of common sense. Of course, governors of the Fed are not the only ones in Washington to have come to this conclusion; there have been enough characterizations of Paul Volcker as "the second most powerful man in America" to ruffle many a feather in the executive branch roost. And action is being taken; nominations to the Federal Reserve Board are quickly becoming as politicized as nominations to the Supreme Court, and for the same reason. By far the most interesting development to watch in Washington in the coming years will be the evolution of the relationship between the Fed and the rest of the power structure.

Money, America's Business

America's most vital import is and has alwaws been money. This was true, as we saw, two hundred years ago, and it is still true today. Because of its huge domestic resources and markets, America could, if necessary, function without most imports. It produces more than enough food to feed itself, and it could, at a cost, dispense with such staples of contemporary business as foreign oil, coal, silicon, steel, and paper. However, if foreign capital stopped flowing to America's financial markets, it would be a catastrophe because of the number and magnitude of the ensuing bank failures. America can survive any embargo except an embargo on money. This is why the issue of third-world debt has caused more worry than OPEC-led oil-price increases: Whereas being cut off from OPEC oil only means higher oil prices, an interruption of payments by Mexico, Brazil, or Argentina would mean a huge reduction in America's money imports.

This cuts both ways. The rest of the world can pretty well do without most of America's exports, even without its food surpluses, as China is now in the course of demonstrating. But the world would be at a loss without American money and money expertise. By most every measure of power and achievement, the United States comes out second best, at most: China has a bigger potential domestic market, Japan and Korea can build better and cheaper family cars and consumer electronics, Europe produces better sports cars, art films, and designer clothes, Russia has a stronger military, Switzerland has more stable banks, and Scandinavia a higher standard of living. But there is one thing which America does best: creating and moving money.

The very onslaught on traditional businesses by strict money interests, the most visible of which are the corporate raiders, the takeover artists, the greenmailers, and the junk-bond wizards, is a sure sign that business has strayed from its core business, making money, and that America has let it get away with it. During the days of the dollar standard, America was entrusted with the world's money; it flunked the test because it thought that its business was to run the world with the same nationalistic priorities as other nations had put forward in the past. Adherence to the myth that the business of America is business has been the first big mistake of America; this is understandable, since there are no precedents for the American experience, for an entire continent to be into money, not into business. Provided we come to grips with this reality, the wildest dreams can come true; the sky can once again be the limit.

Money Myth 6:

The Inescapable Logic of Money Is That Some People Will Always Be Poor

THE MYTH: Money, by its nature, is undemocratic and excludes the lowest rungs of society from access to wealth. Money increases the discrepancies between the mighty and the weak. Money, like other commodities, is a finite substance and there is only so much of it to go around: every limousine on Park Avenue means that many more hungry children in Harlem. The implacable logic of money is that, as money accumulates in some places, poverty inevitably increases, not only in the ultra-poor continent of Africa but at the very heart of American society.

The Myth in Action

Seeing money as a kind of inherently limited-size pie leads to two equally detrimental conclusions. Some consider that it is simply futile to address the problems of inequality and distribution of wealth, since those problems are caused by money itself and are therefore totally intractable, even with the best of intentions. Meanwhile, others simply decide that the most expeditious way to achieve social justice is to more or less arbitrarily redistribute whatever wealth and money is already around. The first group considers anyone concerned about inequality as an incurable utopian, while the second bunch treats those opposed to their redistribution schemes as stubborn, narrow-minded opponents of the eradication of poverty.

A common reflex brought about by the idea that money implies that some people will inevitably be poor is to conclude, "Better them than us." This is the starting point of a string of beggar-thy-neighbor attitudes, the most typical of which is that of certain business people who insist on perpetuating the tradition of the nineteenth-century robber barons and strive to get rich by cutting the wages paid to their work force to the lowest possible level in order to keep more money for themselves.

The Myth Unraveled: Money Does Not Create Poverty

The situation of blacks in America, the financial straits of farmers, and the seemingly inextricable poverty in Africa are often cited as proof that the logic of money means wealth for some and poverty for others. However, we are going to show that none of these phenomena are due to money, but are the result of an entirely different set of causes, chief among which is money illiteracy and the attempt to sidestep the logic of money. Moreover, a good case can be made that the modern way to make a lot of money is precisely to spread it around.

Money is not responsible for poverty. Poverty is caused by the absence of money, by limitations placed on the growth of money, as a result of the combined efforts of a number of social forces, including the actions and attitudes of those who claim to represent the best interests of the poor.

A Sadly Informative Case History:
Black America

The single most obvious failure of the American Dream is the continuing economic plight of the blacks. Blacks have failed to close the income gap, making 53 percent as much as whites in 1948 and about the same percentage in 1973. In 1983 three times as many blacks lived in poverty as whites, while the number of blacks classified as poor increased from 31 percent in 1978 to 36 percent in 1983, according to the U.S. Bureau of the Census. In other areas there has been a more marked regression.

> The proportion of one-parent, female-headed black families increased from 18% in 1950 to 33% in 1973. The proportion of blacks on welfare also rose during the 1960's and 1970's. . . . The proportion of the black population that is working has been declining both absolutely and relatively to whites. Unemployment among blacks has risen, also absolutely and relative to whites. Black teenage unemployment in 1977 was more than five times what it had been thirty years earlier.[1]

The usual conclusion of politicians, sociologists, and psychologists is that blacks are poor because the most intense and long-lasting discrimination to affect any group in the United States has deprived them of political power. This analysis concludes that blacks are in a special situation which requires a unique political solution. This political solution has taken the form of electing black mayors, governors, and congress men and women with the ultimate goal of a black in the White House, and the implementation and enforcement of civil rights legislation, employment quotas, welfare rights, etc. Yet more black politicians and more political programs have made little or no difference. Even in those areas of the country where blacks have risen to political prominence and have therefore theoretically opened up decent opportunities for employment, progress, if there is any, is piecemeal and often short-lived. The reason for the failure of this political agenda is that it fails to address the central issue: money literacy.

The black experience in America has been character-ized by emotional suffering and disenfranchisement. But, more tragically, some 10 percent of the American people were deprived of the opportunity to make and use money. Lack of money has become such a fixture of ghetto life, and making money so alien to this environment, that succeeding at it often leads to ostracization. Successful blacks frequently find themselves cut off from the black community, because they are seen by poor blacks as sellouts playing the white man's game; on the other hand, they are hardly ever fully accepted by nonblacks of com-parable income.

Blacks as a group have been exposed to the worst possible money education administered by the worst pos-sible teachers using the worst possible pedagogy. This pitiful money tutelage began on the plantation; the essence of life there was that blacks never got their hands on money. The people who had money, the planters, offered a feudal role model, pretending it made sense to make money without putting it into general circulation. Money was directly equated with privilege and therefore the province of a limited few. One concrete result of this lack of money experience was that "the economic weighing of necessities against luxuries which was common and taken for granted among other peoples of the world, was some-thing that slaves in the United States had not experi-enced for centuries. . . . For generations, on into the twentieth century, black leaders themselves repeatedly complained about the wastefulness, extravagance, or improvidence of their own people."[2]

Graduates of the plantation school of money moved on to the often racist world of labor. On the plantation money was not seen as a source of repression, since it remained basically inaccessible. In the factory blacks' perception of money changed. They were traditionally paid lower wages than their white counterparts and were used as a means to control labor unrest; their miserable condition made them ideal strikebreakers and union disorganizers. Money was seen as a white man's game in which they were pawns. These factory owners continued the on-the-job money disinformation started by the planters, promoting the notion that once again money was the property of a privileged group whose power stemmed from their good fortune at being born with white skin. And it was commonly believed that anyone who wanted to make a lot of money simply had to be, or was bound to become, as greedy as the employer.

In the 1930s along with the other poor, unskilled workers, blacks found themselves on the government payroll either as employees, first in public works projects and later as soldiers, or as recipients of various forms of aid. From 1941 to 1945 the government was the major employer of poor people; the armed services gave many people their first regular nonfarming jobs. The money lessons learned serving the government in those days were especially detrimental to the money education of an entire generation, since it made it easy to believe that money was something the government could create and hand out at will like some kind of universally accepted food stamp.

The illicit moneymaking activities such as gambling, drug dealing, and prostitution which flourish in the ghettos made a certain sense given that blacks had been systematically denied other avenues to wealth, but though money changed hands, the rackets did not bring major changes to the economic life of the community. Criminal fortunes are nearly always made at the expense of others. Racketeers' superprofits do not enrich the community with the creation of a new product or service; rather, they deplete it financially and physically. Besides, criminality, rather than allowing blacks to go beyond the lessons learned in the government school of money illiteracy, actually reinforced their ties with government. No matter how independent of the law the criminal may seem, his actions are totally defined by their opposition to the law. He is constantly on the lookout for the police either to avoid being caught or to hand out the proper bribe to the proper person at the proper place and time; he devotes a lot of energy to evading taxes. The penal system, the inevitable destination of most of these illicit money-makers, is the logical extension of the criminal's government-centered approach to money. Instead of encouraging new money attitudes, of pointing to new, nonillicit ways to approach money, prisons offer a return to the plantation, a world of slave labor and brutal taskmasters, rigid and irrational hierarchies, graft and corruption.[3] Not surprisingly, after the prison experience, most ex-convicts are not able to make money without resorting to crime, and they inevitably return to jail, where they get a refresher course in bad money habits.

Now that "equal opportunity," job quotas, and school integration and busing are out of political fashion, most of the current business-oriented plans for overcoming the institutionalized poverty of blacks and other minorities rely heavily on the development of small, "minority"-owned, usually service-oriented businesses. This approach is doomed from the start; it ignores the historical process by which such mom-and-pop businesses were wiped out by the first wave of corporate growth: larger businesses usually offer a better product, lower prices, and conscientious product support and after-sales service. As one such venture after another bites the dust, the awful, age-old lesson of resignation will be reiterated: the logic of money is that we will always be poor.

The American Farmers

After the trash-littered ghetto street, the second most common image of poverty in America today is probably that of the heartbroken farm family standing by as an auctioneer sells off their bankrupt homestead. The struggle of the American small farmers has generally been presented as that of decent folk pitted against the irrational forces of both nature and the market. They have been seen largely as victims of circumstances beyond their control, trying to make the best of a situation they did not create. The miserable situation of many small farmers is largely of their own making; it is due chiefly to their devotion to outdated values, which in the end amount to little more than proud refusals to acknowledge the importance of money. Thomas Jefferson elaborated the philosophical underpinnings of the American farmer's money illiteracy. By equating property holders with freemen and freemen with democrats, he established the notion that owning property was a political activity more important than making money, and that in some way it was a threat to the rural life.

> Dependence [not owning property] begets subservience and venality, suffocates the germ of virtue, and prepares fit tools for the designs of ambition. Generally speaking, the proportion which the aggregate of other classes of citizens bears in any state to the husbandmen ... is a good enough barometer whereby to measure its degree of corruption.[4]

From the outset, despite the American farmers' aspiration to become a new landed gentry, there was a vast difference between the relative independence of landowners in Europe and the American farmer's close ties with government.

> The notion rooted in American pseudo-folklore that "free" land left the American a self-dependent individual hardly accords with the facts. In more settled societies like England, where landed wealth had been appropriated by individuals long centuries before, a man received his land through the generosity of his lord, his landlord, his father, his grandfather, or his brother. The American contrast was striking. Here, though the scope for individual initiative in securing land was greater than ever before, the direct help of government was also newly important. Only a government could convert possession into ownership.

No wonder, then, that in America—where everybody,
or nearly everybody hoped to become a landowner—
everyone looked to the government for some personal
benefaction.... They expected the government ...
to help make and keep their land accessible and to
help increase its value.[5]

Until the twentieth century farmers and ranchers did
not need to be very productive to survive; agriculture
was largely oriented toward self-sufficiency rather than
toward the marketplace. Farmers did not see their future in developing agriculture as a business, but in the
permanence of their occupation of a piece of land under
government protection. For all their rhetoric of independent ways, the farmers were much less adventurous than
the merchants, traders, and city folks they so despised. In
business, simply being the first one to come up with a
given product does not ensure permanent or even lasting
dominance of a market. Sooner or later someone came up
with a better and/or cheaper mousetrap. However, the
cardinal rule governing the appropriation and use of land
was something else altogether.

Clan Clubs [local associations of landowners] and
their Clan Club law expressed a distinctive spirit, an
enduring legacy to the new nation. They stood for the
priority principle, which simply meant the superior
claim to those who arrived first.... The principle of
pre-emption, of rewarding the man who got there
first, lasted at least until the end of the nineteenth
century.[6]

Farming could not escape commercialization forever.
The commercialization of farming demonstrated the marginal moneymaking potential of the typical American family farm. "Though 65% of farmers owned farms in 1900,
overall returns to agricultural labor and capital did not
compare favorably with most other economic activities
in the United States."[7] The government had given farmers
their property rights and had protected them against

Indians and trespassers so their reflex was once again to turn to the government for help. Hence the formation of the strong farm lobby, which to this day remains one of the most powerful in Washington. From the very beginning the debate over government support to farmers was never whether the government should give the farmers help but only how much.

The farmers and their lobby had such political clout that it soon became an article of legislative and regulatory faith that "farmers as individuals were at a disadvantage in dealing with other groups and needed the centralizing power of government to place them in a stronger bargaining position." In 1899 the annual budget of the Department of Agriculture was $2.8 million. By 1917 it had soared to $28 million.[8] Nineteen thirty-three saw the establishment of the price support system and of government loans to farmers; for the first time the government, under the First Agricultural Adjustment Act, paid farmers not to produce. The government became the family farmer's banker, financial adviser, and technical expert all rolled into one. It became standard procedure for farmers to be told how much land to till, what crops to grow, and what price to charge for their produce.

World War II and then the Cold War only increased the dependence of farmers upon the government. Agricultural supplies had been essential to feeding the Allied armies, and now pictures of bursting silos in the Great Plains were America's best propaganda against the Russians. This was the height of the idea of the family farm as the basis of America's strength. In fact, the farmers were only buying themselves future trouble because of their blind confidence in the government's advice to keep buying more and more land, even when land values inflated during the seventies; farmers were encouraged by the government to further mortgage their farms and to expand their acreage. When land values and crop prices predictably crashed, the typical farmer was left holding an unenviable bag of rapidly shrinking equity and rising mortgage payments. Probably nothing more clearly illustrated the money illiteracy of the farmer in this era than his trust in the government's investment advice.

Today the small farmer is seen by fewer and fewer Americans as worth saving, largely because the taxpayers are reluctant to foot the bill for bailing out people who have neither the ability nor the inclination to come to terms with money. The only convincing argument for continuing farm support would be to show that farming is a sound business proposition, but for too many farmers, "a farm is not an investment, you do it for security so you will always have some place to go to."[9] Many even offer the financial failure of many farmers as proof of their merits, as the demonstration of how different they are from bankers and professional farm managers, who do not care about the land and only seek to make money. But for just about anyone without a vested interest in the perpetuation of the impasse, the firm reorientation of farming toward making money is the solution to the plight of the farmers; this would lead to more efficient production and eventually to cheaper and more abundant food, and would go a long way toward putting an end to the world's food imbalances.

Africa

While hunger is being successfully beaten back just about everywhere, even in India and China, the situation in Africa is simply getting worse. While per capita income is showing signs of improvement in most of what is commonly known as the third world, that of Africa remains stagnant. There may be a lack of money in Africa, but there is no lack of interest in money. The signs of a fascination with money are everywhere: people flood cities like Lagos looking for money, and those who are able to get visas emigrate, preferably to America, and never come back. The overwhelming poverty of Africa is the result of Africans having been subjected to an even more comprehensive campaign of money illiteracy than American blacks.

Africa was saddled with a double layer of money illiterates: the colonialists and the traditional power structure.

The money role models available in Africa were even worse than those presented by the southern planters in the United States. By and large, the European colonialists were the most incompetent business people of their time, adventurers who could not have been succesful in their own country and who did not dare try their luck in America. They generally gave money a bad name because of their exploitative practices and primitive techniques of social engineering.

The traditional African leadership, the tribal chiefs, unlike early American black leaders, had a vested interest in preventing the spread of money. They felt directly threatened by money because it encourages independence from the traditional values, which are the basis for traditional authority, and because it provides a more effective means of resolving social problems than does mysticism. In a primitive, premoney society the gods and their earthly representatives, the spiritual specialists, were responsible for the magic acts of transformation necessary to sustain life. They disappoint as often as they come through, and the failures of the gods to deliver require elaborate and often contradictory justifications. But money is more consistent (money is nothing if not consistent), more accessible (no secret rites or special training necessary), and infinitely more democratic. Unlike the old ways of tribal society, money doesn't require arcane rites and exclusion; it appears as a straightforward, no-nonsense proposition, especially to the young. Compared with the traditional rites of passage, the initiation of money is painless and open to anyone. Yet money retains some of the magical quality of the spirit world, since it has a certain omnipotence and elicits universal recognition. The chiefs, and later many in the African intellectual elite, encouraged the identification of money with the colonial and neocolonial regimes, with the white man's world, presenting money as something quite alien to Africa.

The damage was only compounded by the professional politicians who came to power when the colonialists, unable to stand the heat, hurriedly got out of the African kitchen. The new leadership seemed to divide their time between attacking money and looting the national treasury, in a strange populist mixture. Idi Amin Dada enjoyed a degree of popularity all over Africa largely because of his onslaught against money, mostly in the form of attacks of Uganda's Indian and European community as well as on any black Ugandan who showed signs of affluence. He gave the confiscated businesses to his cronies, who, not having the slightest idea how to run a business, could find nothing better to do than sell off the inventories and close up shop. Mobutu Sese Seko, the president of Zaire, preached the gospel of antimoney asceticism; his favorite slogan was, "It is better to die of hunger than to be rich and a slave to colonialism." Of course, he did not really follow his own advice: it is estimated that he amassed some $5 billion in his personal foreign bank accounts, more than enough to extinguish his country's foreign debt. Julius Nyerere, the former head of Tanzania, made sure that nobody made real money in his country: "anyone earning more than $30,000 a year is in the 95% tax bracket."[10]

Although it may seem otherwise, in the long run nobody interested in making money has benefited from the conditions which have resulted in financial morass and widespread hunger in Africa. The Africans, who for the most part were capable of feeding themselves before the colonialists created one-crop economies, were clearly the victims of the miserable money practices of the colonists. They were saddled with miserably organized, unbalanced economies which contributed heavily to their impoverishment. But in their own way, the Europeans who colonized Africa have paid a price for their money stupidity. Though England, France, and Belgium created commonwealths to facilitate economic relations with their ex-colonies, these relations have come to almost nothing. The chief legacy of colonialism has been the multiplication of largely artificial national political structures which are a major obstacle to the circulation and growth of money. Through their own doing the Europeans have deprived themselves of the possibility of having Africa as a real trading partner, as a genuine source of wealth.

Model Ts, Computers, and the Decline of Social Inequality

Not only is the poverty of such perennially disenfranchised as the Africans, the American blacks, or the small farmers not in the least attributable to any inherent trait of money, let alone to a "logic of money," there is a marked tendency for money to fight social inequalities. More than any other place, America has been the proving ground for the notion that it is possible for individuals to become wealthy, and incredibly so, not at the expense of others, but along with them. At its best, the American way of making money thrives on the idea that the more widely industries disseminate money, the more everyone benefits.

Most historians agree that America has undergone two major industrial and technological revolutions since the 1920s. The typical product of the first was the mass-produced automobile; the computer was both the driving force and the symbol of the second. These two products and the industries built around them changed just about everything about business and work, from the organization of the workplace to the urban landscape, and, above all, they made a lot of people very rich. But this wealth depended essentially on the spreading of wealth and of moneymaking opportunities and skills to vast numbers of people, many of whom were only remotely connected with those businesses.

Henry Ford and the Twilight of the Wobblies

Henry Ford was one of those rare historical figures who, before undertaking what will become their major achievement, are able to describe exactly not only what they are going to do but what the consequences of their work will be.

Ford's announcement [of the Model T] contained as little grace as the thing he was talking about. "I will

build a motorcar for the great multitude," he said
pompously. He went on to remark that the Model T
would be so low in price it would be within the
means of everyone. . . . In 1909 Ford's idea was revo-
lutionary. In that era motorcars were generally considered to be ostentatious toys of the wealthy.[11]

How Ford managed to make his cars affordable was
as remarkable as the very affordability of the car itself.
More than the assembly line, the central element in Ford's
scheme was to put a lot of money in as many pockets as
possible. In an age when most industrialists generally
conformed to the portrait of the robber baron, doing
everything to keep wages low and their own earnings as
high as possible, Ford proposed to make his own workers
and, by force of example, ordinary workers everywhere
full-fledged consumers with money in their pockets. This
was the logic behind the bold introduction, in 1914, of
the famous five-dollars-a-day wage scale at the Ford plants.
It has been said that "this announcement created a
sensation greater than the outbreak of World War I. . . .
the wage of five dollars for eight hours for common labor
was twice as much as the highest common labor wage in
the United States."[12]
Ford had turned the industrialists' logic on its head. In
his own words: "Industry must manage to keep wages
high and profits low, otherwise it will limit the number
of its customers. One's own employees should be one's
own best customers."[13] He recognized that if business was
to fully enter the twentieth century, it would have to
overcome the notion that money could only be made by
leaving behind a trail of poverty, social injustice, and
resentment. In the process he contributed mightily in
breaking the deadlock in the debate between the equally
unrealistic robber barons and their utopian opponents.
His confidence in the ability of money to provide a
viable alternative to the wildly skewed income distribution of the robber barons' era led to a head-on collision
with his own stockholders, who were demanding the kind
of exorbitant dividends typical of nineteenth-century industrial ventures.

Instead of dividing ten million dollars among the
stockholders . . . Ford proposed they get along with
1.2 million. The stockholders went to court to force
Ford to distribute the company earnings. At the trial
Ford told the court that the profits . . . were neither
his nor the stockholders'. "After the employees have
had their wages and a share of the profits, it is my
duty to take what remains and put it back into the
industry to create more work for more men at higher
wages." He denied that either generosity or his conscience had anything to do with it. It was simply
good business.[14]

When the court ruled in favor of the shareholders and
ordered the payment of dividends, Ford resigned in protest. Then he quickly proceeded to buy out the company's
entire stock, taking the firm private. It seems that even
here, Ford could not stop spreading wealth. Whereas a
Cornelius Vanderbilt would probably have exerted vengeance (he is known to have written to some associates
who had crossed him,"I shall now proceed to ruin you,"
which he promptly did), Ford, even though he had profound differences with his stockholders, nevertheless made
them very rich. Each one of them became a multimillion-
aire when Ford bought them out.[15]

While Ford's five-dollar day and the massive reinvest-
ment of profits incensed the old-style tycoons and investors, these innovations practically put the radicals and
utopians out of business. The lines forming outside the
Ford factory were not picket lines, but waiting lines for
one of those five-dollar-a-day jobs. The Model T had also
given mobility to the workers; this in itself was a hedge
against poverty and the arbitrary decisions of the industrialists. Workers were no longer faced with the dismal
alternative of either putting up with miserable conditions
or getting beaten up or killed in desperate protest actions; the new worker, with a little money in his pocket
and a Model T could move himself and his entire family
in search of a better situation if conditions so dictated.
Even some of the most vehement traditional opponents

of business recognized Ford's contribution to the cause of social justice.

> Archie Sinclair, an organizer and editor for the IWW, a crew not given to kind words for industrialists, hailed Ford above Marx. "Agitators from John the Baptist to Earl Browder have made a lot of noise but accomplished little. . . . The man most responsible for social progress is Henry Ford."[16]

Computers and Underdevelopment

In the early 1970s the state of the computer industry was similar to that of the automobile industry before Ford. Computers were essentially reserved for a small number of users consisting mainly of large corporations, universities, and the government. The industry itself believed that the evolution, both of computers and of the market for computers, would be a slow, more or less incremental affair. The idea of a computer for the masses was as foreign to this line of thinking as that of a car for the masses had been half a century before to the suppliers of luxury touring cars.

What the pioneers of the personal-computer industry did was to bet on the public's intelligence. This time, it was not a matter of putting money into people's hands; this had been accomplished by Ford's revolution. Rather, the idea was to offer the public a product which would, in essence, be a device for saving time and money.

Like the Model T, the personal computer has not only brought great wealth to those who developed it but has also tended to spread wealth greatly. New jobs, products, and services were created by the wide availability of inexpensive and powerful computers; by the same token a lot of repetitious, boring work was made faster and better, if not eliminated altogether. Small companies and even individuals were able to create new markets or to make successful inroads in old ones previously dominated by large corporations who had access to pricy mainframe and mini computers.

The computer explosion also addressed one of the prime

causes of inequality on the world level: the concentration not only of money but of know-how in the industrialized countries. The traditional high-technology industries had been unwilling to export expertise for fear that it would foster low-cost competitors and literally put them out of business and their workforce out of their jobs. But in the highly competitive personal-computer market, locating not only the rather simple tasks of assembly but even the production of components abroad became a necessity. This meant more money and more knowledge circulating in places which had until then been relegated to the role of purveyors of junk merchandise. South Korea, for example, went from being a manufacturer of relatively unsophisticated consumer electronics products like television sets and video-cassette recorders to being a full-fledged producer of inexpensive, powerful micro computers within a short few years. And nobody in the computer industry seems to resent the fact that much since the resulting fall in computer prices will likely bring in a whole new group of consumers, which in the end will mean more money for everyone.

Toward Money Literacy: Using Money to Make Poverty Visible and Measurable, and Getting a Handle on It

Money does not cause inequality and it does not contribute to the perpetuation of it. On the contrary, money tends to force us to address the problem of inequality because it makes inequalities visible. Money is the yardstick which allows us to measure the extent to which ideals of justice and equality are implemented. Before money, poor people had no clear notion of how poor they really were. Serfs and slaves had a general notion that there were a few aristocrats and prelates who were very wealthy, but they could not formulate and communicate this difference in a clear and concise fashion. The same phenomenon can still be observed in this day and age in countries with little or no money, or where money plays only a marginal role in everyday life because of the prevailing political system; people in such countries have no means of measuring inequalities and therefore have a very hard time trying to deal with them. The very presence of money is a step toward more justice. Unlike the majority of Africans, who live in essentially moneyless societies, the blacks of South Africa, who get paid wages to work in the mines and who must pay for their groceries, know not only that they make five, ten, or fifty times less than whites but also how far they have to go to reach true equality; they know how much money they would have to come up with, if the country's economy were for sale, to buy their freedom from the society that now holds them captive.

In the eastern bloc countries there may be widespread suspicion that party bosses, senior military personnel, and other upper-level bureaucrats are much better off than the population at large, but it is next to impossible to measure by how much, since only a small part of the upper classes' privileges consist of financial advantages. In the Western world, on the contrary, it is relatively simple to tell how much better off the Rockefellers, for instance, are than the bag lady on the corner. Here, where everything has a clear price tag, poverty is anything but invisible. Whenever and wherever privileges can be expressed in terms of money, the abyss between rich and poor is clear (indeed, surveying the abyss is a growth industry that includes the Michael Harringtons and their vivid accounts of disenfranchisement as well as the chroniclers of the life-styles of the relatively rich and famous and the various compilers of who's richer-than-who lists).

By allowing the measurement and quantification of social phenomena and problems, money gives us a handle on them, in the same way that our system of weights and measures gives us a handle on physical phenomena. As the great British physicist Lord Kelvin put it: "I often say that when you measure what you are speaking about, and can express it in numbers, you know something about it; but when you cannot measure it, when you cannot express it in numbers, your knowledge is of a meager and unsatisfactory kind."

Those who blame poverty on money do not only commit the mistake of blaming the messenger for the bad news but also deprive themselves of any way to understand and solve the problem.

————Money Myth 7:————

Money Is Materialistic and Vulgar

THE MYTH: Money induces insensitivity and selfishness; it makes people oblivious to the needs of others, since making money implies disregard for the most elementary standards of ethical behavior. The pursuit of money distracts people from the pursuit of the higher, more noble values usually identified with religion and the arts.

The Myth in Action

The moral character of anyone who "makes it big" is suspect; it is assumed that being financially successful requires stepping over somebody, if not systematically, then at least somewhere down the proverbial road. It is taken for granted that one must "sell out," sacrificing one's moral principles and/or esthetic ideals, in order to make money. This notion is so deeply ingrained that even the most token proof that one did not part with all integrity and intelligence on the way to success is usually sufficient to turn one into a cult figure: the media regularly report how this or that person is amazingly honest, moral, or a great artist in spite of all the money he or she has.

The first result of this belief is that many people simply

stay away from any substantially profitable activity for
fear that it will somehow demean them; this is the perennial rationale and excuse of starving artists, inventors,
and geniuses. Worse, this leads many among the poor to
accept their miserable condition by fostering a false sense
of moral superiority, something like, "We may be poor
but we are honest, decent, and caring folks, unlike the
rich." The complementary effect is, of course, the flood-
ing of the marketplace with shoddy goods and unimagi-
native services, the dubious courtesy of people and businesses who are sure that in order to succeed, one must be
mean, immoral, and dishonest and cater to bad taste.

The quintessential art form of the twentieth century,
cinema, with its unique mixture of art, culture, and business, offers one of the best opportunities to see this myth
in action. At one end of the spectrum lies the no-money
world of the struggling art film directors, committed
documentary filmmakers, and actors intent on not com-
promising their art, while at the other end lies Hollywood, its questionable glamour, and its myriad scandals.
Here, except for a few pets kept on a longer leash like
Woody Allen and, in the past, Orson Welles, formulas
rule, in an industry dominated by culture vendors who
can always justify their behavior by paying lip service to
high culture.

Like any industry, Hollywood spends a good deal of
time analyzing why people buy its product. The reasons
can be reduced to two: story and stars. According to the
movie industry, the average person wants a simple, reassuring story that fits in a genre and follows a formula.
The industry in general, and the executives in particular,
prefer to think that they are giving the masses what they
want—low culture—which makes big money because it
suits the common taste. This is a self-fulfilling prophecy
which boils down to this: the masses have mass taste.
The movie industry fervently believes that real culture,
high culture, is superior to money and above the understanding of the average person. The more money Hollywood makes peddling drivel, the more this view is
confirmed, hence the usual justification: the industry is

not responsible for the general vulgarity and the dismal artistic and intellectual content of the movies, since it only responds to the market and to the imperatives of moneymaking. Moreover, the perpetrators of low-brow films regularly atone for their sins by supporting "real art": movie people are compulsive buyers of paintings and other artifacts of high culture, while commercially successful stars often work for low wages on art films. See, they say, when an obscurely made film on an obscure topic bombs, we told you, art doesn't sell. They should add, "and we love it because it doesn't sell."

Money and Selfishness

In the September 2, 1984, issue of *The New York Times Magazine*, John Kenneth Galbraith offered his comments on what was then the hot topic of social commentaries everywhere, the "phenomenon" of the rise of the "yuppies." Rather than referring to the yuppies by using that familiar, vulgar acronym, Galbraith enlarged the concept and spoke of the "newly affluent—blue-collar workers with middle-class incomes, the new, vastly enhanced professional class, the modern, relatively well-paid white-collar bureaucracy, those protected from the trials of unemployment, old age and illness." Galbraith berates this money-centered generation in no uncertain terms: "Their political tendency is that of the affluent of the past. It reflects the age-old capacity for ignoring or rationalizing the differing fortunes of the rich and the poor."

Galbraith's moralizing is typical of what may be called the secular version of the ancient religious curse on money and affluence. But Saint Paul's celebrated warning that the love of money is the root of all evil seems quite restrained when compared with the wholesale condemnation of money by contemporary moralists. Today's preachers, clerical as well as secular, have dropped all qualifiers and boldly state that money itself, and not merely the love thereof, is the root of all nonethical behavior, that there is a fundamental contradiction between the logic of money and decent human behavior. In some of the more bizarre interpretations, money is even shown to stand in the way of happiness. New variations on these themes are offered every day by the various contemporary champions of morality, from the Pope and the ayatollahs all the way to television's soap operas and police dramas. Money, the Great Satan, is everywhere: it does not merely drive people to murder and larceny, it perverts the very core of human nature. Money's inescapable side effects are greed and ruthlessness; money makes people insensitive to the suffering of others. Money is not only accused of acting as the awful catalyst for crass (and mass) materialism, it is castigated as synonymous with irretrievable vulgarity, as in the Bob Dylan lyrics, "money doesn't talk, it swears."

Money is widely blamed for the current sorry state of contemporary art, religion, and social involvement. In the case of art, money is cast as the villain in the alleged debasement of contemporary art: the art scene is said to have been turned into a speculative circus managed by cynical agents and gallery owners and by artists more concerned about controlling the supply of their works than with nurturing the creative spirit. In the realm of religion, the worldly belongings of the Catholic Church are widely blamed for that faith's theological impasse, and the greed of such sectarian leaders as the Reverend Moon is legendary. Money, more than anything else, is held responsible for having killed the "spirit of the sixties," a period acclaimed as a high point of social commitment and compassion.

The underlying assumption is that there are higher moral codes and values, promoted and preserved by religious creed, political institutions, patriotism and art, which somehow save us from the evils of money. In spite of the constraints imposed by money, there remain a few great artists who carry on the pursuit of esthetic truth in bohemian obscurity and who struggle against the vulgarity of a world whose sole concern is money. Dedicated politicians and other social reformers have their work cut

out for them righting the injustices money has created, compensating for the selfishness and complacency,
public and private, which money reputedly brings about.
Religion is a kind of refuge of last resort: when the modern believer invokes his or her God, the prayer uttered no
longer implores deliverance from the fury of the Norse-
men, but from the modern furies of money.

The often scornful distrust of money is not restricted to
the more or less progressive crowd generally referred to
as being "on the left." The ideologues of the "right" are
just as quick to revile money and the materialism it
allegedly fosters. This is especially true of the thinkers of
the so-called new right, who praise the achievements of
the Western economies and the current so-called revival
of traditional values, but who ascribe these successes not
to money, but to work, family, and patriotism, rolling all
three together in a mishmash they call "the spirit of
enterprise." The same goes for heroism. However appealing it was in its no-nonsense reference to money, the line
"No bucks, no Buck Rogers" in the movie *The Right Stuff*
had little to do with the original, Tom Wolfe idea of the
"stuff." Wolfe's original right stuff was a kind of blissful,
vaguely patriotic disregard for money which drove underpaid test pilots to behave like gods. According to this
vision, money is not only vulgar, it is a hindrance and a
bother, a limitation which has to be overcome by a renewal of the frontier spirit. No matter what sector of the
political or philosophical spectrum one turns to, contemporary social reflection appears to be stuck with the par-
adigm of the radical incompatibility of money on the one
hand, and the most fundamental elements of human de-
cency, such as compassion and the quest for justice, on
the other. To quote Galbraith again, "What is not in
doubt is that affluence strains our resources for enlightened compassion . . . one effect of affluence is a continuing conservative trend in politics, and those who dismiss
the pro-affluent movement of these past years as a temporary departure from some socially concerned norm are
quite wrong."

The Myth Unraveled: The Broken Promises of Art, Religion, and Politics

The world of politics, religion, and the arts is generally considered to be ruled by higher standards of morality, compassion, and commitment to the community than is the world of money. The honest, dedicated politician, the holy man, and the artist with a vision, all present themselves as a cut above mere money men. The promise of politics, art, and religion is that of a community based on higher values, of a better life where selfish instincts are transcended. Ever since the Renaissance, the world has witnessed the periodic emergence of would-be innovative artistic movements bent on "freeing creativity" and on promoting the sharing of esthetic experiences. Over the centuries, religion has been offering the promise of liberation, either through contemplation (like Buddhism) or by way of millenarian, communitarian, and utopian visions (as presented by some of the more messianic strains of the Christan or Islamic faiths). The most alluring promise of religion is the promise of freedom from money. Typical of these promises is Isaiah 55:1, "Ho, every one that thirsteth, come ye to the waters, and he that hath no money; come ye, buy and eat; yea, come, buy wine and milk without money, and without price." Similar mirages have traditionally been evoked by power-hungry politicians who, from Pericles to Hitler, rose to power promising freedom and the redistribution of wealth (of course, Churchill promised nothing but blood, sweat, and tears, but he had no choice; besides, he didn't really mean it).

The history of religion, art, and politics reads like a tragic and endless series of broken promises. It offers the sad chronicle of how those religious, artistic, and political movements, when they did not simply dissolve into insignificance and irrelevance, like the communist movements in America, degenerated into exclusive and exclusionary clubs devoted to the exercise of power over their followers and to the tracking down and eradication through persecution (and often physical torture and wholesale murder) of discontent and dissidence. The inquisitorial methods of the papist, antipapist, and other factions of Christianity are notorious, as are the book-burning habits of the most vociferous trends of Islam, such as Shiism. Artistic attempts at "freeing the imagination," such as surrealism, or more recently the cultural phenomena summed up by the term "punk," no sooner surface than they become artistic dogmas, perpetuating the age-old surrender of identity implicit in the adulation of the "masters." And the awful, and generally unavoidable, aftereffects of politics are well known; if all political movements do not have such disagreeable and repugnant consequences as Hitler's Reich, Napoleon's Empire, or Lenin's or Mao's Revolution, they nevertheless always fail to effect the changes which they solemnly commit themselves to when they are making their bid for power. Politicians invariably break their most solemn engagements, whether they promise more or less justice, cleaner air or cleaner politics, more or less defense, or lower deficits; modern politics could be described as the fine art of breaking promises and getting away with it.

While art, politics, and religion promote sharing, compassion, and understanding, they inevitably resort to exclusion, foster privilege, and spawn hierarchies. To varying degrees, individuals involved in any of these enterprises must toe the line of the group's orthodoxy as defined by the higher-ups and/or by tradition; to deviate from this, or even to question the orthodoxy, means living in constant fear of summary dismissal and exclusion. Even for the obedient and the faithful, the fall from grace constantly looms, a most unenviable fate, since such a fall is usually irreversible and without appeal: one is excommunicated from the ranks of "the chosen," purged from the ranks of the "politically correct," or finds out that he or she is no longer considered part of the artistic or ideological "in-crowd." Dissenting members of the Politburo, independently minded Catholic priests, or researchers of Mormon history, all live in constant fear of summary dismissal.

The leaders and exponents of political, religious, or

artistic movements love to speak in terms of absolutes: absolute beauty, absolute justice, absolute spirit, absolute good and absolute evil; the beatniks lived in a universe of absolute cool and today's punks in a cosmos of absolute negativity. Even today's most commercially inclined esthetes regularly see themselves as mediums charged with the mission of bringing the absolutely obtuse masses in contact with the absolute esthetic truth. The playwright Peter Schaffer, hyping the upcoming movie made from his play *Amadeus*, wrote: "Of course, great art always attests to the existence of absolutes. . . . Not to be vague, the creation of the *C Minor Mass* or the final act of *Antony and Cleopatra* seem to me to give a point to evolution: most human activities don't."[1]

The artist claims that he or she, thanks to his or her own privileged gift of insight and expression (submission to the whims of producers or gallery owners are seldom mentioned as part of what it takes to reach the public eye), can communicate this absolute, or at least some fraction of it, to a public, the members of which live generally meaningless lives in the transient, finite, money-bound world of the relative. Commenting on the tendency of the newly affluent to buy works of art, New York artist Jim Cherry states it quite candidly: "Yuppies have money beyond the house, the BMW, and the baby. They want to buy meaning for their lives. And where do you buy meaning? They look to art."[2]

In their own way, religion and politics make the same claims to confer some kind of absolute meaning which is otherwise missing in everyday life. Today's growth religions generally promise the sharing of some secret which will bring, if not fulfillment, at least some relief from the guilt and angst usually associated with the monetary consequences of both failure and success. Indeed, religion spends a lot of time and energy trying to convince as many perfectly normal, successful, and relatively happy people as possible that modern life is frightening, horrible, immoral, and devoid of significance. This is the basic message of the papal visit-type religious extravaganzas, which become truly obscene when the Great Man speaks to the members of his flock in Latin America or Africa and unflinchingly tells the (usually) cheering crowds that people in the developed countries are just as unhappy as they are, and even more so, since they are plagued with too much money, and the more money you have the further from God you are. And this great truth is corroborated by televised illustrations of the personal distress and moral decreptitude of the rich and famous. The artists who concoct such antimoney parables as *Dallas*, *Dynasty* and *Miami Vice* join (however unwittingly: after all, to them, it's only a gig) hands with religious preachers and political leaders to reinforce the myth that the more money you have the more miserable you are. From the Everglades to the Texas oil fields, money brings moral turpitude, psychological instability, and all-around meaninglessness.

The Broken Promises of Business: Business Gives Money a Bad Name

When politicians, artists, and religious leaders heap blame on money, their charges are generally taken with a grain of salt, since they come from a point of view essentially and visibly different from that of money and moneymaking. More damaging to money's reputation is that business, which is generally identified with money, shares in some of the manipulative and exclusionary practices of art, politics, and religion.

Beyond individual business personalities' adhesion to a given religion or cult or to specific political doctrines or parties, there is a fundamental tendency of business to think of itself, or to pass itself off, as a religion or even an art form. At Commodore during its heyday, Jack Tramiel's business doctrine was referred to as "the religion." Any number of business people, large and small, like to think of themselves as world conquerors and empire builders in the cast of Napoleon or Julius Caesar; one of Canada's most successful newspaper publishers is rumored to pay

homage regularly to a bust of Mussolini which he keeps
in his office. The notion is that making money is not
essential, because after all it is quite vulgar and not even
worth mentioning; what gives meaning to the million-
aire's life is that he or she transforms the world and is
guaranteed a place in history. Corporate culture is a
constant concern of most businesses, and attempts to
enforce adherence to it are often reminiscent of religious
inquisitions or political witch-hunts. Corporate conven-
tions, especially those geared toward the sales force, look,
sound, and feel disturbingly like religious revival meetings or political rallies, complete with fire-and-brimstone
admonitions from the higher-ups about the corporate
hell that awaits those who don't proselytize zealously
enough. And boosters of the "entrepreneurial spirit" sound
even more like preachers and politicians than do their
corporate counterparts; they often profess a yen for the
ascetic, self-flagellating side of life, to the extent of
never taking a day off or going on holiday ("To me, my
business is everything").

A common trait links the exponent of corporate culture, the self-proclaimed entrepreneurial maverick, and
religious, artistic, and political preachers: they are peddlers of meaning. The first, indispensable step in the
recruitment of converts to the business mystique, corporate or entrepreneurial, is to convince people, through
arm twisting, blackmail, or plain old-fashioned repetition and browbeating, that their lives are devoid of meaning without the company or without a small business of
their own. And since money is obviously at the central
element in people's lives, the promise is not so much of
money, but of money with a bonus, money with meaning;
the rallying cry of the peddlers of meaning is "Money
isn't everything!" A particularly gross example of this is
the direct-sales business, where joining an army of door-
to-door peddlers is presented as a major, qualitative improvement in one's existence, as the access to financial
independence. Here the product being offered is meaning
in life, no less: Amway, the direct-sales giant, presents
itself as the defender of the "American Way." In the same

vein, the boosters of entrepreneurism insist that venture capitalists are "more than mere money men," that they are visionaries who have a unique knack to help translate new concepts into reality.

Like artists and politicians, business leaders often endorse religion; many of them are staunch backers of religious fundamentalism. When the American Catholic bishops came out with the first drafts of their pastoral letter on the economy, Catholic business personalities (including the formidable William Simon and the ever witty Al "I'm in charge here" Haig) sprang to the defense of traditional church doctrine on business, typified by the laissez-faire approach of the Boston and Chicago dioceses: let the police keep the order, the businessmen make their profits, and the church get its tithe; the rest will fall into place.

Business people support the artistic worldview in at least two ways: They support artists financially through direct grants, contributions to foundations, and commissioning works of arts that reflect their "corporate culture"; William S. Paley, a compulsive collector of art, commissioned the fabled "Black Rock" CBS headquarters, possibly the most famous monument to a corporate culture. Second, business likes to think of its activity as inherently artistic. Like the artist, the enlightened entrepreneur, most often working in solitude, creates an original masterpiece which he then struggles to bring to the world, overcoming the doubts and ignorance of lesser humans. When finally recognized for what it is, a masterpiece, the world becomes a better place forever.

Almost every business, from the most obscure small business to the more visible and vociferous Mobil Oil and W. R. Grace concerns, is into politics and social issues, trying to prove, mostly to itself, that "despite our money, we are still concerned with the quality of life, the budget deficit, the standards of education, and the nation's state of readiness to stand tall and face up to the Red menace." No matter how much it depends on money, business is basically scornful of money, just as art, politics, and religion are. At best, business people seem to be saying,

money can buy redemption (if you give it to a worthy
cause, to support some charity or church) or meaning (as
in art), or it can be lavishly spent to promote business-
oriented reforms disguised as lofty ideals (as in politics),
but it is seldom if ever publicly acknowledged to be the
number one concern, the true mover and shaker, a perfectly legitimate motive in itself. Those who publicly admit that the pursuit of money is their main motive and
guideline are usually presented as avaricious and immoral, especially if they are successful in business. Donald Trump, the real estate developer and promoter, is the
scourge of New York largely because he neither disguises
his activity nor makes excuses for it.

Yet business, despite all its tendencies to behave like
art, religion, or politics, is never as elitist or as manipulative because it is closer to money in its day-to-day functioning. Business simply cannot afford to be as blatantly
contemptuous of people as religious leaders, demagogic
politicians, or avant-garde artists are. No director of marketing would dare insult his customers by referring to
them as "my flock" while portraying himself as the
"good shepherd" the way holy men do, or billing himself
as "the great communicator," as is popular among
modern-day politicians and artists. Money polices the
world of business much more closely than it does the
realms of art, religion, and politics, because business is
the one activity which cannot take place without money:
art can exist in the abstract, in the concept of the esthetic
experience, which has nothing to do with money. The
same goes for the religious experience, which in its "pur-
est" forms is essentially not of this world. And politics is
probably the most abstract of all, being the pursuit of
raw power. Business, on the other hand, cannot exist in the
abstract; no matter how hard one tries to imagine something like "pure business," one cannot conceive of business
without money; and business leaders who have religious,
artistic, or political ambitions are often reminded of this
basic truth: a business person's only interesting feature is
his relationship with money. In order to remain interesting,
to wield any kind of lasting influence, business people must
conform themselves, at least in part, to the ways of money.

Money and Business Ethics

Businesses which bet on the existence of stupid, sheepish consumers invariably suffer. In the 1970s energy suppliers of every kind (most notably OPEC, but also every kind of utility, gas, hydro, or nuclear) bet that people would continue to be foolish in their use and misuse of energy, much in the same way that Detroit bet that the passion for shiny gas guzzlers would never abate. These proved to be singularly bad bets. The smart money said people would get smarter, and they sure did, for their money's sake. Though this may sound simplistic, it is what happened. Whereas years of protest by ecologists had resulted in absolutely no progress, when the effects of the energy shortage were translated into money terms, solutions were rapidly forthcoming.

The high-tech industries are not immune from the tendency to underestimate the intelligence of consumers. This attitude has brought misfortune to the promoters of Videotex, a system of home data retrieval, who insisted on selling people terminals and dedicated software which only allow access to grade-school-level predigested drivel to which the label "data bank" has been hastily affixed. For about the same price as that of the Videotex terminal, people can buy a whole computer, a "smart" modem, and open-ended communications software, none of which presumes stupidity on the part of the end user. Videotex ventures which treat the user like a nincompoop are bound to keep meeting with consumer rejection.

Retribution for the underestimation of public intelligence does not stop at the door of the exploiter of public credulity; it goes all the way to the investors and the banks which financed its operation. Business cannot afford to be dumb and monolithic, any more than it can get away with regarding its customers as dummies. And the closer to the immediate handling of money a business is, the more perilous being stupid or insensitive to the outside world is. Banks, which are undeniably the businesses closest to money, are especially vulnerable in this respect, and even more so now, in the era of modern, global money. As chairman Isaac of the FDIC said: "In the old days, an ordinary bank *couldn't* fail, it had to be incompetent or crooked first. Now all you have to do is to make some dumb decision."[3] Major banks are now in financial straits, not because they came up with a few wrong projections of growth for the energy or the high-tech industries, but more fundamentally because they bet on public stupidity. In the case of loans to Poland, for instance, they assumed that the Polish population would forever take abuse from the ruling communist oligarchy; it seems that it never crossed the Western bankers' minds that the Poles could someday paralyze the country's industry and thereby jeopardize the repayment of the nation's loans simply because they wanted some money and some consumer goods to spend that money on. This same logic of counting on the docility and subservience of the citizenry led the same bankers to lend indiscriminately to South American dictatorships, with even more serious results.

Ever since Vance Packard published *The Hidden Persuaders*, we have been living with the notion that marketing and advertising are overwhelmingly powerful manipulators of public opinion. But the all-manipulative, all-powerful ad, the business version of political or religious brainwashing, is nothing but a myth. The point has been made quite convincingly by Michael Schudson that ads "have only the most happenstance and eclectic theoretical foundation; they are not based on any serious understanding of people's attitude about world goods."[4] This is a lot more consistent with the actual practice of advertising, not to mention the level of intellect of advertising people, than the traditional Vance Packard–derived theories of thought control which describe manipulation by advertising that borders on conspiracy. As Mark Vamos puts it, "Detroit was devastated by the Japanese not because Honda Motor Co. and Toyota Motor Corp. figured how to advertise to the save-the-whale crowd but because Japanese cars were demonstrably cheaper, sturdier, and more fuel-efficient than American cars."[5] In any case, the most successful advertising seems to be that which follows the introduction of a product which is destined to be a success because it already has a market, an audience, to which it is responsive. And simply calling a product smart is not sufficient; no amount of marketing can make up for a stupid product or stupid evaluations of the consumer's needs. To quote from the "religion" according to Jack Tramiel: "The key to running a company is not marketing. It's how you design and buy."

Toward Money Literacy: The New Morality of Money

The charges of vulgarity and crass materialism leveled at money by artists, politicians, and religious people are self-interested lies. These people hate money because money has the uncanny ability to expose the pettiness, corruption, and greed which characterize so many of their lofty enterprises. The money dealings of politicians, church leaders, and artists are very often less than exemplary and, unlike many other questionable aspects of their behavior, they have a tendency to become public. The scope of the Watergate scandal was due more to the size of the money shenanigans of the Committee to Reelect the President than to the questionable political activities of the White House "plumbers." As Reagan's former budget director, David Stockman, put it, "If the SEC had jurisdiction over the executive and legislative branches, many of us would be in jail."[6] The Reverend Moon knows this from firsthand experience, having enjoyed the hospitality of the local jailhouse, and the Vatican has yet to recover from the Banco Ambrosiano scandal, which almost landed its chief financier, Msgr. Paul Marcinkus, in the same predicament as Mr. Moon. And the good reputation of the art world has hardly been enhanced by the questionable commerical practices of even such venerable auction houses as Christie's and Sotheby's. Money relentlessly and mercilessly exposes the seamier side of politics, religion, and the arts and brings their less appealing traits out in the open in such a way that cannot be ignored. This is why politicos, preachers, and creators excoriate on money, and there is a kernel of truth to their antimoney ramblings, protestations, and admonitions: money is indeed totally alien to their way of doing things.

For centuries, religion has been bogged down in morals; most people are quite confused about the difference between morals and religion, a confusion adroitly exploited by religious fundamentalists: for instance, if you don't want indiscriminate abortions and pornography over the airwaves, then get religion (the Jerry Falwell line); or, if you don't want a corrupt government run by foreigners, then get religion (as in contemporary Shiism). Clearly, this kind of religion is far too busy meddling in worldly affairs; it has no time left to devote to its basic concern, the spiritual. It can be argued that up until now, religion had to be involved in defining and enforcing moral standards because nothing else could. Today, however, money not only lays down the day-to-day standards of conduct but also provides the incentive to abide by them and ensures swift punishment when necessary. Religion no longer has to offer a comprehensive code of behavior, like the Koran or the Torah; the ethic of money is no longer Protestant, it is universal, and quite unlike the Protestant Ethic. Religion can now concentrate on spiritual and theological pursuits. Money not only frees religion from the management of secular morality but forces organized religions to clean up their financial act. Nostalgics of the era of religion may deplore this, since it loosens their grip on society and forces them to question their traditional positions of power, but one thing is certain: over the years, money has done more to improve the ethical standards of religion than religion has ever done to civilize money.

Conclusion

The Rise of Money Literacy

As we have seen, the consequences of money illiteracy are far-reaching and ominous. Money illiteracy is at the root of many of our major social problems ranging from the poverty of the blacks to the decline of the small farmer to the semipermanent state of war and insecurity which haunts us. Money illiteracy undercuts the attempts of many individuals to achieve success and even makes them feel guilty if and when they do succeed. Money literacy and money-literate attitudes, on the other hand, are undeniably appealing; they are definitely an asset, since individuals who manage to transcend the money mythology understand what money is and what it does, and as a result are better equipped to make sense out of this world and to function in it. In a world dominated by money, money literacy is a must for everyone, whether or not one is intent on making a lot of money. Nobody can afford to be illiterate money–wise or ill at ease with money.

Given the intrinsic value of money literacy, it is hard to imagine anyone who would be opposed to it. But as we have seen, the yuppies, who are often among the most open to money literacy, have aroused a vociferous opposition, largely because their approach to money suggests some fairly sweeping social as well as personal changes which put into question the status quo and the livelihood of a number of people. One way to measure the magnitude of these implications is to observe how those who administer and who interpret our major social institutions have responded to the money approach of our generation.

The Official Story

Nowhere is the determination of social scientists to suppress the importance of money and of the growing money literacy more obvious than in the history they have collectively written of our own generation, a history which has been endorsed by many among us. When money appears in historical accounts, it is largely as a negative force, a source of corruption and conformity which people either succumb to or reeact against depending on largely arbitrary circumstances. The chronicles of our generation, of the world since World War II, are largely written as a series of abrupt reversals, of radical self-negations, of tragic and inexplicable contradictions. According to these accounts, whether written by Herbert Marcuse or Daniel Boorstin or compiled weekly in *Time* magazine, the postwar generation has no discernible center, no mature set of priorities, and is largely a group of well-intentioned but lost sheep attracted to a series of spectacles, causes, and issues by celebrities, political leaders, and gurus, and guided by a kind of fickle and whimsical but fundamentally crass materialism. In our opinion the best way to understand anything about our own generation in our own day and age is to look at recent history from the point of view of our contemporaries' main avowed preoccupation: money.

We have been unable to find a history of modern America, whether from the right or from the left, which does not align corporate America, bureaucracy, and money on one side of the barricades and radicalism with its humanist bent for social change on the other. The pop sociology descriptions of the last few decades sum up this herky-jerky journey: the fifties are presented as a period of tranquil acceptance and apathy (the age of *Father*

Knows Best), the sixties as a time of political activism and youthful rebellion (as enshrined in *Hair*), the seventies as an interlude of self-examination and self-indulgence (as in *Bob and Carol and Ted and Alice*), and the eighties as the return of the conflict between self-indulgence and compassion. But a history of the last thirty years focused on money and money-related changes looks very different from this official story.such a history conveys all the excitement and promises of our times.

The Fifties: No Big Sleep

The 1950s were purportedly a time of calm, complacent prosperity when nearly everyone, except for a few virulently anticorporation and antimoney bohemians, like those weirdos of legend the beatniks, went along with the quiet pursuit of the American dream. The period is invariably presented and perceived as an era of social stagnation presided over by Eisenhower, that benignly senescent father figure. Closer examination reveals that, rather than being a perfect model of social passivity, the fifties were a time of intense change centered around money.

In the late 1940s America, having come out of the war as the world's richest nation, was not only, for all practical purposes, entrusted with the administration of the international monetary system but also had to give a massive transfusion of money, know-how, and competent personnel to countries like Germany and Japan in order to make them fit trading partners again. As a consequence, Americans, who were not exactly known for their cosmopolitan worldview, began to think of themselves as international beings rather than as plain folks because so much of the world looked to the United States both for a model of material progress and for the financial resources necessary to achieve it. By the beginning of the fifties, Americans and their money were everywhere and were remodeling the world's way of life. In return, this movement of people and of money brought a new wave of foreign, particularly European, influences, though this time without the foreigners moving to America. For all the complaints of nationalists, especially in Europe, about the heavy-handed imposition of the American way of life, in reality the main feature of the fifties was that America itself was becoming more cosmopolitan than ever. Americans were eating Chinese food, drinking French wine, buying German cars, wearing Italian clothes, and decorating their homes with Scandinavian designs.

The most noticeable development on the domestic front was the social reorganization created by the growth of suburban communities. Today the surburbs are usually described with disdain; they are pictured as the embodiment of what is least appealing in traditional American values and as the symbol of the destruction of our nation's open spaces by the profit motive. It is very difficult nowadays to find defenders of the suburbs outside the real estate and construction industries. But the suburbs, the development of which was only made possible by the unprecedented affluence of the middle class, including blue-collar workers, did make an important contribution to social progress. Gone in one fell swoop were the old city neighborhoods with their rigidly defined ethnic and religious loyalties and their formal laws of social encounter. The suburbs provided an affordable escape from the stultifying family ties of the extended family and also challenged the orthodox practices of traditional religion. Of course, new patterns of more or less typically suburban conformity did emerge, as the chroniclers of mass society were quick to point out. But whatever the level of passivity, the celebrated obedient spectator of this era, typified by the Weeji photograph of the movie audience wearing 3-D glasses which appeared on the cover of *Life* magazine, was no more obedient than the participants in mass culture today. The dramatic changes in the tastes of consumers, the dislocation of the traditional social landscape, and the general monetarization of life, combined with the demographic impact of the baby boom, meant that the social reality was approaching critical mass. People did not simply wake up one fine morning in the mid-sixties to decide life was unlivable and then drop out. The seeds for the widespread questioning of values and ways of life during the sixties were planted in the changes centered around money which took place in the fifties.

The World Since the Sixties: Toward Mass Money Literacy

By the 1960s the new generation was getting acquainted with the business superstructure, either through early work experience or through college and university education, which was and is essentially geared toward the needs of business and government. It soon became apparent that the profound social changes which had affected every major aspect of American life outside the workplace had had very little effect on business practice or on the way future employess were trained. The corporate clock had stopped in 1941 and hadn't budged since. The universities were trying to educate a generation schooled in a rapidly evolving process of modernization to conform to what industry ordered—more men and women in gray flannel suits. The confrontation between the aspirations of the rising generation and this regimented world was all but unavoidable.

The crisis which triggered the protest movement of the sixties had little to do with such political issues as civil rights, the relative merits of the belligerents in Vietnam, or the legalization of various mind-altering substances. The real issue was the condition of the modern individual in America; the attack on the university was essentially a critique of a bureaucratized society and its inherently rigid governmental and corporate apparatus. The protest movements was not essentially a student phenomenon; it was the expression of a powerful, broadly based demand by young people for the right to determine their own future free from the inflexible corporate and governmental structures. Their demand for "fulfilling" lives was a demand for the right to make money on their own innovative terms, and it was echoed by young people throughout the world. Unfortunately, the headline-grabbing tactics of the antiwar movement overshadowed these more fundamental issues, as the threat of the body bags turned the political debate over the draft and Vietnam into a life-and-death issue.

Eventually, most of the ex-activists and countercultural drop-outs joined the workaday world of businesses big and small, or of self-employment. In the seventies most started earning more money than they had ever earned in the public or countercultural sectors, and they spent most of it on themselves and on their families rather than using it to further causes they no longer believed in. Almost to their surprise, they discovered that making money was a challenging and fully satisfying activity.

It was not so much that an entire generation had come to the brilliant realization that money had become the new agent of revolution, and was using it with a vengeance. It is more accurate to say that there was a return to the issues raised in the mid-sixties, this time with a fuller awareness of what society was and how it worked. This generation gradually realized that more significant and longer-lasting change was being affected by money than by any voluntarist attempt at reform; it was able to realize, for instance, that the superstrong dollar of the early 1980s has done more to advance the technological and manufacturing abilities of developing nations than all the aid packages and anti-imperialist programs, marches, and coups put together. The years of the "super dollar" have seen the realization of the conservative American industrialists' nightmare: the exporting of factories and technological know-how to foreign countries at a rate never seen before. The irony is that even the most nationalistic, beggar-thy-neighbor industrialists have to spread money and knowledge all over the world simply in order to remain marginally competitive. This is what happens, to a greater or lesser degree, every time an American corporation transfers manufacturing overseas. This process has encouraged the rapid modernization of a number of countries, generally improving social conditions, and in a certain way has put an end to the plight of the traditional immigrant, who no longer has to leave Korea or Taiwan or Singapore to enjoy many of the benefits of America, such as the acquisition of technical skills, which can only translate into more money for more people.

Our contemporaries are also able to recognize that a year or two of expensive insurance premiums imposed on businesses which persist in irresponsible practices has done more to curb environmental pollution, unnecessary surgery, unsafe toys, and dangerous pharmaceuticals than all the letter-writing campaigns, protest marches, and legislations combined. And they can see that wars are fought on a smaller scale today, not because the peace movement has finally touched the heart of the world's military, but because war has become increasingly expensive to wage, and people increasingly reluctant to foot the bill for them. Until this generation started judging politicians according to money criteria, despots like the shah of Iran were condemned solely for their violations of civil and human rights. The maimed and wounded were paraded as proof of the inhumanity of a tyrannical regime while the despots issued sweeping denials. The shah's ill-gotten fortune of several billion was simply ignored by political critics. Over the last seven years a dramatic change has taken place. Today an autocrat like Ferdinand Marcos is not judged primarily by how many of his political opponents he may or may not have murdered. There is a general consensus that a more accurate measure of his ineptness is provided by how much money he looted from the national treasury and how poorly he managed what he did not steal. While the shah could deny that he ordered torture, and even find some moral justification for it if necessary, the Marcos family is unable to dispute the size and origin of their money improprieties.

Money Illiteracy and the New Politicians

The new breed of politicians who are rising to national prominence are engaged in a competition to demonstrate whose program is the most money-smart, because in today's political scene the politician with the best line on money is very likely to be one who is elected. From David Stockman to Newt Gingrich to Bill Bradley to Jack Kemp, Washington is filled with urgent talk about balanced books, the values of privatization, the virtues of the free market, the most bang for the buck, and the social cost of the national debt, while the local political scene everywhere is teeming with reformers and cost-rationalizers of every political creed. And there is every evidence that the same thing is happening throughout the world; even the rulers of Russia and China now insist on the necessity for reforms and economic efficiency. On this face evidence it would seem that even politicians have come to acknowledge the need for government to conform to the imperatives of money, to shed its money illiteracy. But rather than contributing to the growing body of working knowledge on money, the new politicians, like their predecessors, pay only lip service to money, actually relegating it to the back seat and reinforcing money illiteracy. From the founding fathers to Ronald Reagan, American politicians have claimed that they were not only knowledgeable about money but essential to its creation. They and their counterparts around the world have fostered the notion that prosperity depends not simply on the stability of political institutions but on social immobility. But as we have seen throughout this book, the expansion of money is inseparable from social change, and politicians have little to do with these changes; if anything, they tend to prevent them and severely limit their impact.

Our generation has definitely upset the cozy world of intellectuals, politicians, and traditional business, not so much by being antimoney, as so many of us thought we were when we dropped out altogether or protested against various injustices supposedly caused by money. Our biggest challenge to money illiteracy was to take the promise of economic opportunity seriously and to be outrageously positive about money. By pursuing the promise of wealth with a vengeance, by taking society at its word, we have put traditional money wisdom on the spot, forcing a revision of most of the assumptions about wealth held by old-line money experts and businesses, and discarding their stodginess and conservatism as obstacles to moneymaking and to money literacy.

Money and Maturity

Currently, the baby boom generation is reaching maturity. In most accounts of human development, adulthood is characterized by a realistic appraisal of one's strengths and weaknesses and a willingness to use strengths and to come to terms with weaknesses. The paradox of this generation is that both our strengths and weaknesses lie in money and in our relationship to it. The strength of our generation is centered around our growing money literacy, yet this strength is tempered by a willingness to accept the aspersions cast against us by money illiterates; our main weakness stems from our hesitation to get rid of the vestiges of money illiteracy we still carry with us and which actually hinder both our ability to deal with money and our ability to understand and shape the world around us and our own lives.

New Orleans, Paris, Berkeley, Montréal, New York
1984–86

ANNOTATED BIBLIOGRAPHY

Athos, Anthony, and Pascale, Richard. *The Art of Japanese Management*. New York: Warner Books, 1981.
Like all books on Japanese business, this one assumes that Japanese-style manufacturing is *the* way to make money and then proceeds to berate American business for lacking the cultural values that allow us to conform to this view. The sad thing is that many Americans agree and are moved to flagellate themselves publicly for the creation of what is generally a more progressive and enlightened society.

Bach, Steven. *Final Cut: Dreams and Disasters in the Making of "Heaven's Gate."* New York: Plume/New American Library, 1986.
Published in 1985, this is a revealing history of an artist gone mad because he lost touch with reality, i.e., money.

Bamford, James. *The Puzzle Palace*. New York: Penguin Books, 1983.
The state of the art of communications interception and high-tech snooping as of 1982. If you think that we overstate the government's obsession with secrecy, read this one. Also rife with details on the relationships between the intelligence community and businesses like Western Union, RCA, and IBM, pointing to a more than uneasy relationship.

Barro, Robert J. *Macroeconomics*. New York: John Wiley, 1984.
Hailed by many, most notably *The Wall Street Journal*, as the hottest economics textbook around. Actually quite readable, but unfortunately a prime example of Robinson Crusoe-ism.

Beard, Charles. *An Economic Interpretation of the Constitution.*
New York: Macmillan, 1936.
Beard's book, though intended to demonstrate the inherent
unfairness of the Constitution, is as much a tribute to the
ability of money to upset the apple cart as anything else.

Bell, Daniel and Kristol, Irving (eds), *The Crisis in Economic
Theory.* New York: Basic Book, 1981.
Interesting collection of articles by economists of just about
every hue. Not breathtaking, but gives a good glimpse of the
kind of debate going on among economist.

Boorstin, Daniel. *The Americans.* New York: Random House, 1974.
Boorstin's trilogy *(The Colonial Experience, The National Experience, The Democratic Experience)* contains a wealth of information on the fabric of everyday life in America over three centuries.
His explanations for the development of our social structures
tend toward the simplistic. Number one among them seems to
be the sheer size of America.

————. *The Lost World of Thomas Jefferson.* Chicago: University
of Chicago Press, 1981.
Boorstin, who as librarian of Congress must have read every
book in the world, has turned out a very important and readable little book which points out the many differences between
the Jeffersonian's worldview and ours, and should keep us from
making any hasty equations between their times and ours.

Bracken, Paul. *The Command and Control of Nuclear Forces.*
New Haven, Conn.: Yale University Press, 1983.
Should be read by all those who think they understand nuclear
strategy, especially by the no-nukes set. Quite technical, but
shows the extent to which the military does not know what to
do with its nuclear arsenals.

Bretton, Henry. *The Power of Money.* Albany: State University
of New York Press, 1980.
Despite its somewhat moralistic point of view, this scholarly
book is a good starting point for the study of the effect of
money on politics and government.

Carr, James. *Bad: The Autobiography of James Carr*. New York: Dell Books, 1975.
A straightforward and unapologetic account of a life of crime and of the brutal prison system which perpetuates it. This book represented a huge step beyond *The Autobiography of Malcom X*, since Carr offered his own raw and scathing criticism of radicals and do-gooders, black and white; he was killed for it.

Clarfield, Gerard H., and Wiecek, William M. *Nuclear America*, New York: Harper & Row, 1984.
Probably the best compilation of the nuclear follies; somewhat less partisan and definitely more comprehensive than most. For instance, you may have forgotten that there were once plans to develop a nuclear-powered plane (imagine a meltdown over O'Hare or La Guardia) and that the inspiration for Star Wars, the ever witty Edward Teller, once said that either atmospheric radioactive fallout would have no effect at all on the environment and its inhabitants or that its effects would be beneficial.

Clausewitz, Carl von. *Campagne de 1799 en Suisse et en Italie*. Paris: Champ Libre, 1979
———. *On War*, New York: Penguin Books, 1982.
The first of these is an interesting study of how war was waged in the Napoleonic era without Napoleon (the French commander in chief was Masséna; Bonaparte, meanwhile, was getting beaten in Egypt). The second, of course, is the classic book of strategy; that it should be considered a challenging work by the military is more indicative of the limitations of military thinking than of the intrinsic depth of the work. All those who think that a belief in the superiority of strategic defense is something invented by Ronald Reagan and Cap Weinberger will be surprised to find it spelled out here; the rest will not be surprised to see it reheated by those politicians.

Debord, Guy. *The Society of the Spectacle*. Detroit: Black & Red Press, 1970.
First published in 1967 (in the original French, *La Société du Spectacle*, Paris: Buchet-Chastel), this brutal indictment of commodity society and of communism leaves one question unanswered. If we are all spectators, how did so many incredible things get done in this world?

Emmott, Bill, and Pennant-Rea, Rupert. *The Pocket Economist*, New York: Cambridge University Press, 1983.
These two veteran journalists from *The Economist* have turned out a very useful, generally penetrating, and often quite hilarious (*a la* British, of course) "alphabetically guided tour of economic terms, economic institutions, and the world of high finance." Typical of their approach is their definition of money, which starts off: "Replaced barter and cowrie shells, and has been giving trouble ever since." Indeed.

Finley, M. I. *The Ancient Economy*. Berkeley, Calif.: University of California Press, 1973.
Solid, academic overview of the subject.

Fite, Gilbert. *American Farmers: The New Minority*. Bloomington: Indiana University Press, 1981.
Levelheaded appraisal of the causes of the decline of the family farm.

Foster, Peter. *Other People's Money*. Toronto: Totem Books, 1984.
Money illiteracy in the Canadian oil patch. Even the bankers are not so hot up there.

Friedman, Milton. *A Program for Monetary Stability*. New York: Fordham University Press, 1960.
Just what it says.

Friedman, Milton, and Friedman, Rose. *Free to Choose*. New York: Avon Books, 1981.
Standard Friedman pap. There is government (always bad) and the market (always good), and there is the military, which is damned good because it mixes the two. Hey, guys. We know your argument contradicts itself.

Galbraith, John Kenneth. *The Anatomy of Power*. Boston: Houghton Mifflin, 1983.
Galbraith as patriarch: human nature never changes, all organizations are the same, etc. We can't help it: even though we managed to avoid both, we still find a wide difference between

the exercise of power in the military and in the average business concern.

――――. *The Great Crash*. New York: Time, 1954.
Standard reasonable Galbraith.

――――. *Money*. Boston: Houghton Mifflin, 1975.
Due for a revision, but is probably the only good and readable historical overview.

Gilder, George. *Wealth and Poverty*. New York: Bantam Books, 1981.
The ideology of entrepreneurship in all its verbosity. In the cover blurb, David Stockman, who was hot stuff at the time, praised the book as "the best thing on economic growth in 15 years." Mind you, the back-scratching was entirely mutual: in the preface, Gilder, a self-confessed disciple of von Hayek, Ayn Rand, Irving Kristol, Bill Buckley, and the Friedmans, casually mentions that then-Representative Stockman "is by far the leading intellectual in the U.S. Congress." This is monetary-supply-side dogma for the masses disguised as economic theory, the pernicious kind of political rhetoric disguised as money wisdom which the New Right drools over. A typical Gilderism is that women working is bad because it makes their spouses feel "unmanned." Very profound, this.

Goodenough, Simon. *Tactical Genius in Battle*. London: Phaidon Press, 1979.
Illustrated descriptions of famous battles focused, as the title says, on the tactical aspect of warfare. More a coffee-table book than a treatise, but to the point and packed with numbers, something often omitted from more lengthy works. A note to thriller fans: Len Deighton wrote the introduction.

Guillemin, Henri. *Napoléon*. Paris: Trévise, 1969.
A nasty portrait of Bonaparte drawn by France's most controversial historian. There's nothing like it, anywhere.

Halberstam, David. *The Powers That Be*. New York: Alfred A. Knopf, 1979.

At his best when he describes Roosevelt's pioneering efforts at news management and when he draws portraits of Henry Luce of *Time* or William Paley of *CBS*, Halberstam just gets boring when he extols the role of the press in the Vietnam or Watergate affairs. Come on, everyone knows that "working journalist" is a contradiction in terms.

Hammond, Bray. *Banks and Politics in America from the Revolution to the Civil War.* Princeton, N.J.: Princeton University Press, 1957.
The prime source on the subject.

Hanson, Dirk. *The New Alchemists: Silicon Valley and the Microelectronics Evolution.* Boston: Little, Brown, 1982.
Patchy, but one of the few non-personalities-oriented histories of the legendary Valley.

Harrington, Michael. *The New American Poverty.* New York: Holt, Rinehart & Winston, 1984.
Prime Harringtonia. The poor are still poor; Harrington goes back to his old social services haunting grounds and can't believe what he sees. More interesting for what is left unsaid than for its limited perspective on poverty. The problem here is one of basic dialectics: one's views on poverty are necessarily incomplete if one does not also consider the issue of wealth.

Harvard Nuclear Study Group. *Living with Nuclear Weapons.* New York: Bantam Books, 1983.
Who wants to?

Hawken, Paul. *The Next Economy.* New York: Ballantine Books, 1983.
Though it contains a clear presentation of intelligent consumers and of smart commodities, in the end the book is a polemic in favor of the new eco-entrepreneurs and a call for elegant scarcity.

Heilbroner, Robert L. *The Worldly Philosophers.* New York: Simon & Schuster, 1980.
Latest revision of a 1953 classic. You could do a lot worse than to read this one, especially as regards Adam Smith and the changes in economic thinking after him.

Heilbroner, Robert L., and Thurow, Lester. *Economics Explained.*
New York: Simon & Schuster, 1986.
First published in 1982, this is a version of the authors' college
textbook, *The Economic Problem,* aimed at the general public.
The book is dominated by the neo-Keynesian (or whatever it is)
outlook of Thurow and Heilbroner, but at least the authors have
the honesty to acknowledge that "money is a genuinely perplexing and also a genuinely complex subject."

Holbrook, Stewart. *The Age of the Moguls.* New York: Crown
Books, 1985.
First published in 1953, a useful reminder that the "moguls"
were not a monolithic and unanimous group. Concise and vivid
portraits of those legendary characters.

Internationale Situationniste. *De la Misère en Milieu Étudiant.*
Paris: Champ Libre, 1976.
This tract first appeared in France in 1966; it was an instant
international success, translated as *On the Poverty of Student
Life.* A mean, funny critique of university life which contains
some keen observations on the Free Speech Movement. Marred
by a call for workers' power, whatever that is.

Jacobs, Jane. *Cities and the Wealth of Nations.* New York: Ran-
dom House, 1984.
Cities are essential to the wealth of nations; okay, okay. Like
McLuhan: not that great, but not bad for a Canadian.

Johnson, Paul. *A History of the English People.* New York: Harper
& Row, 1985.
The usual Johnson approach. Merciless criticism of the close-
mindedness and equivocation of the English. Still, he has a
bone to pick with English education, which he sees as the
single most important cause of the decline of Britain. Hard to
believe, really.

———. *Modern Times.* New York: Harper & Row, 1983.
The best account of the last sixty years in print. Falls for
almost none of the ideologies, except that Johnson, despite a
scathing attack on professional politicians, still believes in the

saving power of the enlightened statesman who recognizes his mission is to guide his flock through the troubled currents of history.

Josephson, Matthew, *The Robber Barons*, New York: Harcourt Brace Janovich, 1934.
Even though it to is the line of the classic liberal denunciation of the early capitalists, this book is still invaluable for its vivid description of that era.

Jomini, Antoine Henri. *Précis de l'Art de la Guerre*. Paris: Champ Libre, 1977.
Along with Clausewitz, the other classic writer on warfare in the Age of Revolutions. Many in the military prefer this book to Clausewitz's because it is a lot simpler, more a compilation of tactical recipes.

Keynes, John Maynard. *The General Theory of Employment, Interest and Money*. New York: Harcourt Brace Jovanovich, 1964.
Goes without saying.

Kindelberger, Charles D. *The World in Depression, 1929–39* Berkeley: Unversity of California Press, 1973.
Demonstrates that the money foolishness of the period was a global phenomenon.

Kissinger, Henry. *Nuclear Weapons and Foreign Policy*. New York: W. W. Norton, 1969.
Geopolitical reveries; chills you to the bone.

Lamb, David, *The Africans*. New York: Vintage Books, 1984.
An excellent antecdotal account of contemporary Africa.

Luttwak, Edward. *The Pentagon and the Art of War*. New York Simon & Schuster, 1985.
The self-styled Clausewitz of our era offers what is probably the most devastating criticism of the military on record, but with a difference. While most people consider that the military is a wasteful bunch, but that at least it manages to find a few

good men and usually gets the job done when the shooting starts, Luttwak considers that the waste doesn't matter much because today's military is far too civilian-oriented and incapable of fighting wars (even its one big success of recent years, the invasion of Grenada, is described as a complete bungling act by Luttwak). This book quickly became gospel in Washington, where the generals never read business theory and the politicians never read military strategy. Luttwak knows both. Dangerous! (The recent "raid on Libya" was probably more a response to Luttwak's criticisms, most notably of carrier task forces and interallied coordination, than to terrorist goings-on.)

Manchester, William. *The Arms of Krupp*. New York: Bantam Books, 1968.
Long-winded, but invaluable to help appreciate the difference between European business and business as it developed in America.

————. *American Caesar: Douglas MacArthur, 1880–1964*. New York: Dell Books, 1978.
The American way of war in full regalia.

Mayer, Martin. *The Bankers*. New York: Ballantine Books, 1974.
A detailed account of how the banking system works including its inherent foibles. A bit dated because of deregulation.

————. *The Money Bazaars*. New York: Dutton Books, 1984.
Picks up where *The Bankers* ended.

McClintick, David. *Indecent Exposure: A True Story of Hollywood and Wall Street*. New York: William Morrow, 1982.
Interesting account of money illiteracy and shady deals in and around Hollywood.

McElvaine, Robert. *The Great Depression*. New York: Times Books, 1984.
A decent historical account. Like all books on the Depression, this one has its axe to grind; in this case, it's the liberal, anti-supply-side approach.

Melman, Seymour. *The Permanent War Economy*. New York: Simon & Schuster, 1985.

A thorough indictment of the money stupidity of war. Does not go far enough in tracing the influence of the Pentagon approach on U.S. industry, limiting its effects to the defense sector.

Moffitt, Michael. *The World's Money*. New York: Simon & Schuster, 1983.
Does more or less for the international currency markets what Martin Mayer's books did for U.S. banking.

Morison, Samuel Eliot. *The Oxford History of the American People*. New York: New American Library, 1972.
Liberal, humanist account of American history. Suffers from virtues and weaknesses of condensation, as well as from terminal Kennedyism.

Naisbitt, John. *Megatrends*. New York: Warner Books, 1984.
Everything every critic ever said it was and less. Equates money with information. Popularity of this book in business circles is best proof that business is in trouble.

Okun, Arthur. *Equality and Efficiency: The Big Tradeoff*. Washington, D.C.: Brookings Institute, 1975.
Scarcity thinking at its most Jesuitic.

Peters and Waterman. *In Search of Excellence*. Formulas for those who claim to know that formulas are the problem. Advocates a return to an era that never really existed. Fabricates an entire history to justify its banal solutions.

Phillips, Michael. *The Seven Laws of Money*. Menlo Park, Calif.: Word Wheel, 1974.
Countercultural platitudes parading as money wisdom by the guy who invented the MasterCard, no less.

Pisor, Robert. *The End of the Line: The Siege of Khe Sanh*. New York: Ballantine Books, 1982.
Don't bother with the details of the Westmoreland vs. CBS lawsuits. Read this. Even if you spent hours in front of the box watching the PBS series on Vietnam, read this. If you will not read another book on Vietnam or on war, read this.

Reich, Robert B. *The Next American Frontier.* New York: Penguin Books, 1984.
This book advocating Reich's panacea for the American economy, the adoption of a national "industrial policy," was acclaimed by everyone from George Gilder to Walter Mondale. Ho-hum.

Shultz, George P., and Dam, Kenneth W. *Economic Policy Beyond the Headlines.* New York: W. W. Norton, 1978.
Shultz from his pre–secretary of state days. A true Washington pro, he had been, among other things, secretary of the treasury, and secretary of labor. Dam was an assistant director of the Office of Management and Budget when Schultz occupied what was to become known as Stockman's job. The chapter on international monetary policy is especially interesting, retracing the events surrounding the Great Float of 1971.

Singer, Mark. *Funny Money.* New York: Alfred A. Knopf, 1985.
A hilarious account of how money stupidity perpetuates itself in the banking industry.

Siu, R. G. H. *The Craft of Power.* New York: John Wiley, 1979.
Military thinking applied to corporate warfare and office politics by an ex-honcho of the army's Quartermaster Corps.

Smith, Adam. *The Wealth of Nations.* Chicago: University of Chicago Press, 1967.
Keeps people talking, after two hundred years; but not quite what you would expect, either.

Smith, Adam (pseud.). *The Money Game.* New York: Random House, 1967.
Even though everyone today knows who "Adam Smith" is (a TV personality), it is still interesting to reread this investment strategy book and especially its more general statements about money and economics, mainly because it was one of the early modern pop money-related best-sellers.

Solomon, Robert. *The International Monetary System 1945–1976.* New York: Harper & Row, 1977.
Though it is not the author's intention, this book shows how hard

it is for governments to control the movement of money across borders without suffering dire and unpredictable consequences.

Souvarine, Boris. *Staline*. Paris: Champ Libre, 1977.
Subtitled "a historical overview of Bolshevism," this is the best and most disturbing biography of Stalin. Even more disturbing is how it has been kept more or less out of print since 1940.

Sowell, Thomas. *Ethnic America*. New York: Basic Books, 1981.
Overturns classic liberal thinking on the economic consequences of racial prejudice. Sowell's work is largely unknown outside of academic (and government) circles because his style is dry and his conclusions tend toward the timid.

———. *Knowledge and Decisions*. New York: Basic Books, 1980.
A more conceptual formulation of Sowell's economic thinking.

———. *Markets and Minorities*. New York: Basic Books, 1981.
More about ethnic America.

Summers, Harry G. *On Strategy: A Critical Analysis of the Vietnam War*. New York: Dell Books, 1982.
The complement to Luttwak: obsessed by the notion of "people's war," this professor from the army's War College strives to show that America's mistake in Vietnam was that it did not succeed in making the war popular, something which should be avoided in the future.

Talleyrand, *Mémoires 1754–1815*. Paris: Librarie Plon, 1957.
The memoirs of Bonaparte's Kissinger give irreplaceable clues to the nature of the emerging modern state.

Thurow, Lester. *Dangerous Currents*. New York: Random House, 1983.
Of course, we all know where Thurow stands (on the liberal side of things) and where he speaks from (MIT). Nevertheless, this is more than interesting. Thurow at his best, offering a good, somewhat sarcastic but never condescending summary of current economic thinking. Too bad his criticism remains on a technical, news-analysis, level.

Toland, John. *Adolph Hitler.* New York: Ballantine Books, 1976. Toland may be of doubtful value as a historian, but he is an above-average biographer.

Voyer, Jean-Pierre. *Une Enquête sur la Nature et les Causes de la Misère des Gens.* Paris: Champ Libre, 1976.
Though written in obscure Hegelian prose, this book makes an excellent argument that wealth rather than scarcity makes the world go round. Voyer's slogan, "The economy doesn't exist," is exactly what is sorely missing from Thurow's book, for instance. In any case, it prompted us to look at money, something which does exist.

Weigley, Russell F. *The American Way of War.* New York: Macmillan, 1973.
By the author of the *History of the United States Army* (which we have heard is under revision at the present time), this book is just what it says. Invaluable.

Yardley, Herbert O. *The American Black Chamber.* New York: Ballantine Books, 1981.
In 1931 this book was published as a plea for the reinstatement of intelligence-gathering agencies which had been disbanded after World War I. Its tales of Yardley's spy-catching activities during that war may be somewhat corny, but the book gives a good sense of how small an affair government and national security were barely fifty years ago.

Zuckerman, Edward. *The Day After World War III: The U.S. Government's Plans for Surviving a Nuclear War.* New York: Viking, 1984.
Sensationalistic but nevertheless interesting, especially because it shows the intricacy of the mechanisms planned to ensure governmental control of money even if everything is destroyed. Presumably, the government's real concern is that money could very well get on with the job of rebuilding the world without government, which would be a lot easier than for government to try and do the same without money.

Notes

INTRODUCTION

1. Galbraith, *Money*.
2. *The Wall Street Journal*, August 26, 1985

MYTH 1

1. *The New York Times*, May 4, 1986; Moffitt, *The World's Money*.
2. Thurow, *Dangerous Currents*.
3. *The Wall Street Journal*, December 7, 1985.
4. *The New York Times*, December 12, 1985.
5. Drucker, "Toward the Next Economics," in *The Crisis in Economic Theory*.
6. Jacobs, *Cities and the Wealth of Nations*.
7. Gilder, *Wealth and Poverty*; Galbraith, *The Anatomy of Power*; Smith, *The Money Game*.
8. Podhoretz quoted in Gilder, *Wealth and Poverty*.
9. *The Economist*, May 4, 1985.
10. Drucker, "Toward the Next Economics," in *The Crisis in Economic Theory*.
11. *The New York Times*, February 17, 1985.
12. Quoted in Bretton, *The Power of Money*.
13. Smith, *The Wealth of Nations*.
14. For Robinson Crusoe, see Barro, *Macroeconomics*; for concentration camps, see Sowell, *Knowledge and Decisions*.
15. Thurow, *Dangerous Currents*.

16. Tobin, *The Economist,* April 27, 1985.
17. *The New York Times,* May 26, 1985.
18. *The Wall Street Journal,* May 13, 1985.
19. Ibid.

MYTH 2

1. *The Economist,* October 5, 1985.
2. Ibid.
3. Galbraith, *Money.*
4. Ibid.
5. Quoted in Bretton, *The Power of Money.*
6. Bretton, *The Power of Money.*
7. Mayer, *The Money Bazaars.*
8. Mayer, Ibid., also *The Bankers.*
9. *The Wall Street Journal,* April 30, 1985.
10. *Le Monde,* January 24, 1986.
11. Gilder, *Wealth and Poverty.*
12. Reich, *The Next American Frontier.*
13. Gilder, *Wealth and Poverty.*
14. Bretton, *The Power of Money.*

MYTH 3

1. Boorstin, *The Americans: The National Experience.*
2. Josephson, *The Robber Barons.*
3. Ibid.
4. Morison, *The Oxford History of the American People.*
5. Ibid.
6. Reich, *The Next American Frontier.*
7. McElvaine, *The Great Depression.*
8. Galbraith, *The Great Crash.*
9. Johnson, *Modern Times.*
10. McElvaine, *The Great Depression.*
11. Galbraith, *The Great Crash.*
12. Kindelbeger, *The World in Depression 1929–1939.*
13. Ibid.
14. Halberstam, *The Powers That Be.*
15. McElvaine, *The Great Depression.*

16. Ibid.
17. Ibid.
18. *The New York Times*, February 16, 1986.
19. For a prime example of this line of thinking, see *The Wall Street Journal*, editorial, November 25, 1985.
20. *The New York Times*, January 6, 1985.
21. *The Wall Street Journal*, November 5, 1985.
22. *The New York Times Magazine*, January 13, 1985.
23. *The Wall Street Journal*, January 25, 1985.
24. Melman, *The Permanent War Economy*.
25. *The Wall Street Journal*, May 10, 1985.
26. Bretton, *The Power of Money*.

MYTH 4

1. Goodenough, *Tactical Genius in Battle*.
2. Johnson, *Modern Times*.
3. "In Flanders Fields," poem by John McCrae.
4. Middleton, *Crossroads of Modern Warfare*.
5. *The Economist*, October 5, 1985.
6. *The Wall Street Journal*, February 19, 1985.
7. Melman, *The Permanent War Economy*.
8. Clarfield and Wiecek, *Nuclear America*.
9. Johnson, *Modern Times*.
10. Gwynne Dyer television documentary, *The Defense of Canada*.
11. Clarfield and Wiecek, *Nuclear America*.
12. Quoted in Pisor, *The End of the Line*.
13. Melman, *Our Depleted Society*.
14. *The Wall Street Journal*, October 9, 1985.
15. *The Wall Street Journal*, December 27, 1984.
16. *The New York Times*, March 31, 1985.
17. Luttwak, *The Pentagon and the Art of War*.
18. Ibid.
19. Ibid.
20. Ibid.
21. Figures from Gwynne Dyer's television series, *War*.
22. *The Wall Street Journal*, November 4, 1985.
23. Melman, *The Permanent War Economy*.
24. *Business Week*, February 4, 1985.

25. *The New York Times*, September 1, 1985.
26. *The Economist*, April 27, 1985.
27. Melman, *The Permanent War Economy*.

MYTH 5

1. Hammond, *Banking and Politics in America*.
2. Galbraith, *Money*.
3. Hammond, *Banking and Politics*.
4. Galbraith, *Money*.
5. Ibid.
6. Hammond, *Banking and Politics*.
7. Ibid.
8. Ibid.
9. Ibid.
10. Ibid.
11. Ibid.
12. Ibid.
13. Ibid.
14. Ibid.
15. Ibid.
16. Mayer, *The Bankers*.
17. Galbraith, *Money*.
18. Escott C. Reid, Canada's Undersecretary of State in 1947–48, in an interview with Gwynne Dyer (*The Defense of Canada*).
19. Mayer, *The Bankers*.

MYTH 6

1. Sowell, *Ethnic America*.
2. Ibid.
3. Carr, *Bad*.
4. Jefferson, quoted in Boorstin, *The Americans: The National Experience*.
5. Boorstin, *The Americans: The National Experience*.
6. Ibid.
7. Fite, *American Farmers*.
8. Ibid.
9. Iowa farmer interviewed on *All Things Considered*, National Public Radio, March 18, 1986.

10. Lamb, *The Africans*.
11. Holbrook, *The Age of the Moguls*.
12. Ibid.
13. Ibid.
14. Ibid.
15. Ibid.
16. Ibid.

MYTH 7

1. *The New York Times Magazine*, September 2, 1984.
2. *Fortune*, June 7, 1985.
3. Quoted in Mayer, *The Money Bazaars*.
4. Reviewed in *Business Week*, December 3, 1984.
5. Ibid.
6. Stockman, "off-the-record" speech to the board of the New York Stock Exchange, quoted by *The Economist*, July 13, 1985.